W9-ADB-512

Contents

Editor's Note

By Steve Casper

Dirt biking is probably the most thrilling thing I've ever done in my life. And that's saying a lot since I've been very lucky to experience many different kinds of extreme and fringe sports over the years. However, when I look back at how I began riding off-road motorcycles, I can only cringe when I think about how unprepared I was. Granted, it was pretty much standard procedure back in the 1970s that boys and girls simply learned how to ride minibikes by trial and error, but obviously this was not a very good idea for sports that involve engines, speed, rocks, and trees.

Later in life, I wisely took lessons or attended special schools beforehand when I became interested in other very technical sports such as SCUBA, snow skiing, and even kart racing. Those injections of knowledge and experience right at the beginning benefitted me greatly, and I advanced quickly and safely. Meanwhile, my dirt-biking skills (if you could call them that) remained stagnant for well over a decade. I was always having fun, of course, but looking back now, I never really had a clue what I was doing (even though I thought I was the next Bob Hannah!).

Eventually, I immersed myself in the sport and began riding with expert riders, reading all the tips in the magazines, and studying videos of the top racers. Ultimately, I became a very competent rider and even won a few trophies at the races. But I had to wonder, what if I had had all the right instruction for riding a dirt bike *from the very beginning?* How much quicker would I have become a better rider? How many fewer raspberries would I have peeled off my elbows? How much dough would I have saved in bent levers and broken bars?

It's no secret that finding a local dirt bike riding or racing school is much more difficult than finding a SCUBA or snow skiing instructor. Only a few exist, and one of the most intensive off-road riding schools in the country is called MotoVentures, located near Anza, California. Founded in 1998 by veteran rider, racer, factory tester, and the author of this book, Gary LaPlante, the school has introduced thousands of new riders to the sport in a way that gives them a solid foundation for riding all types of terrain and obstacles and at the same time gives them the confidence to take things to the next level, always in a safe manner.

The MotoVentures course simply follows the tried-and-true methods of learning a technical sport; it begins by laying out the basic techniques to be learned, setting up practice exercises, and then finishing up with real-world practice sessions out on the trails. Over the years, Gary has honed the MotoVentures curriculum into a tight, step-by-step lesson plan that sharply focuses on the fundamentals of riding an off-road motorcycle.

In an effort to offer riders throughout the country the benefits of taking a MotoVentures riding course, LaPlante spent several years putting his entire curriculum for his school down on paper, ultimately resulting in the book you are now holding. You, the reader, can now pour over the many details of exactly how a rider becomes one with machine, then see how to practice each technique with step-by-step photos and instructions. And finally, you'll learn how to apply these principles out on the trails in your next ride with your buddies.

So get ready for one of the greatest adventures of your life as you set out to become a confident, competent, and *safe* off-road motorcycle rider! After all, it is one of the *coolest* sports one can ever do.

Steve Casper
Former communications director for the National Off-Highway Vehicle Conservation Council, and former editor of *Dirt Wheels Magazine*

HOW TO RIDE OFF-ROAD MOTORCYCLES

Key Skills and Advanced Training for All Off-Road, Motocross, and Dual-Sport Riders

Gary LaPlante

motorbooks

First published in 2012 by Motorbooks, an imprint of Quarto Publishing Group USA Inc., 400 First Avenue North, Suite 400, Minneapolis, MN 55401 USA

The information in this book is true and complete to the best of our knowledge. All recommendations are made without any guarantee on the part of the author or Publisher, who also disclaims any liability incurred in connection with the use of this data or specific details.

This publication has not been prepared, approved, or licensed by Volkswagen AG.

We recognize, further, that some words, model names, and designations mentioned herein are the property of the trademark holder. We use them for identification purposes only. This is not an official publication.

Motorbooks titles are also available at discounts in bulk quantity for industrial or sales-promotional use. For details write to Special Sales Manager at Quarto Publishing Group USA Inc., 400 First Avenue North, Suite 400, Minneapolis, MN 55401 USA.

To find out more about our books, visit us online at www.motorbooks.com.

ISBN-13: 978-0-7603-4273 - 2

Library of Congress Cataloging-in-Publication Data

LaPlante, Gary, 1957-
 How to ride off-road motorcycles : key skills and advanced training for all off-road, motocross, and dual-sport riders / by Gary LaPlante.
     p. cm.
 Includes index.
 Summary: "How to Ride Off-Road Motorcycles gives first-time riders all the information they need to know to get started in this exciting sport. Author Gary LaPlante takes riders through a step-by-step lesson plan that details the basic and advanced techniques to safely navigate the trails"–Provided by publisher.
 ISBN 978-0-7603-4273-2
 1. Motorcycling. 2. Mountain biking. I. Title.
 GV1059.5.L28 2012
 796.7–dc23
                                        2012007798

Editor: Steve Casper
Design Manager: Brad Springer
Designer: Bill Kersey

Printed in China

10 9 8 7 6 5 4 3

Warning: Off-road motorcycle riding is an extremely dangerous and sometimes fatal sport. The riders depicted in this book are professionals using proper protective gear and under controlled conditions. Attempting to duplicate their actions may be hazardous. Readers are cautioned that individual abilities, motorcycles, racetracks, terrain, weather, and riding conditions differ, and due to these unlimited factors beyond the control of the authors, photographers, and riders quoted in this book, liability is expressly disclaimed. Do not attempt any maneuvers, stunts, or techniques that are beyond your capabilities.

Foreword

By Lee Parks

If there is one thing that the vast majority of great motor cycle racers and champions have in common, it's that they started riding in the dirt. As for myself, that included both BMX and motocross when I was 12 in 1982. My dad was the one who taught me how to ride in a local field. He didn't have any motorcycle teaching credentials but did a pretty good job with the basics of how to operate a clutch, shift, turn, and stop. Other than that, it was up to me.

After riding for a couple of months, and having more than my share of pizza elbows, knees, and hands, I had my first riding epiphany: protective gear was probably a good idea. I've had many more epiphanies in the following years, all learned the same (read *hard*) way. I would try something new that I saw other riders doing without having any understanding of *how* they were doing it. This trial-and-error method often resulted with me landing on my head—good thing I learned the protective gear lesson early on! Although I eventually became a national road racing champion, these traumatic experiences must have left me with deep psychological wounds if my current career of teaching advanced motorcycle schools (www.totalcontroltraining.net) and manufacturing protective riding apparel (www.leeparksdesign.com) is any indication.

All of this leads us to the book you are reading. A book I will forever hold a grudge toward its author for, for not being out 30 years earlier when I so desperately needed it. The information in this tome on off-road riding could have prevented so much agony and frustration in my life; it's almost too painful to contemplate. Fortunately for you, and future generations, you won't have to learn these lessons the "hard way."

I've had the privilege of calling Gary LaPlante a friend since 1993. He's been an industry insider since I was first learning bipedal locomotion. His MotoVentures school has taught thousands of riders the "easy way" to basic and advanced skills, and we are all lucky that he was able to translate his sizable knowledge into *How to Ride Off-Road Motorcycles*.

While Gary's experience and expertise are indeed impressive, I am even more inspired by his dedication to his fellow riders. We have spent countless hours in person and on the phone discussing how to improve rider training in our own companies as well as systemically as an industry. These conversations are always lively and from the heart and are often abruptly stopped when we inadvertently run out of battery power on our iPhones because we lost track of time. Such is the dedication of a true enthusiast.

There are many things to like about this book: it's comprehensive, based on proven techniques, and even has insightful quotes from some of the best experts in the field at the beginning of each chapter. Additionally, Gary has added dozens of personal "Tales from the Trail" anecdotes that will make you laugh and, at times, cry.

While this book may look cool on your coffee table, don't be afraid to bring it with you to the track or trail. Many of the techniques are best practiced while going back and forth with the pictures and text. I know Gary won't mind if the book gets dirty. After all, that's his favorite pastime.

Lee Parks
Author of *Total Control* and *Race Tech's Motorcycle Suspension Bible*, and president of Total Control Training and Lee Parks Design

Preface

By Gary LaPlante

The book you are now holding is the result of over 43 years of riding, racing, testing, and working on a wide variety of motorcycles. When I founded MotoVentures over 12 years ago, I was able to continue honing my teaching and communication skills by personally training all sorts of riders virtually every week. In other words, I know what works, and what doesn't, when it comes teaching motorcycle riders.

I began riding dirt bikes at the age of 10, growing up as the youngest of three boys riding and racing together as a family in the deserts surrounding Phoenix, Arizona. During those formative years, I competed in a variety of off-road motorcycle racing events including desert races, motocross races, and trials competitions. My father, Ed LaPlante, formed the first trials club in the state, Central Arizona Trials, in 1969. Dad was a visionary who understood the value of riding standing up and keeping your feet up long before he ever heard about the sport of trials, probably out of necessity for riding in the rugged Arizona desert.

Even though they were rare at the time, I had the great experience of attending riding schools as a teenager. These included the Yamaha Learn to Ride Safety Program, the John DeSoto Motocross School, and the Husqvarna/ Rolf Tiblin Motocross School. At one point, I was able to win in just about every type of off-road competition in Arizona,

but I eventually focused on trials and became Arizona State Trials Champion from 1972 to 1975. In 1975, I graduated from high school and immediately moved to California where the motorcycle factories were located and where the best riders in the world practiced and raced. It was very clear to me then that I wanted to make a career in the motorcycle industry.

The following year, Kawasaki Motor Corp., USA, hired me to compete on their KT250 trials bike in the 1976 AMA National Trials Series, where I finished ninth nationally. In 1977, Kawasaki stopped production of the KT250 and canceled their trials support program. However, in 1979, Kawasaki brought me on board as a test rider and mechanic in their Research and Development department working on their popular KX motocross bikes and KDX off-road bikes. A year later, I accepted a new position with Kawasaki's Public Relations department, where for the next six years I was responsible for preparing and accompanying Kawasaki test motorcycles and ATVs that were being reviewed by motorcycle enthusiast media.

In 1985, American Honda Motors hired me away from Kawasaki to work as an engineer in their Product Evaluation department, where I again worked with the press, tested prototype bikes, and created technical briefings and publications for U.S.-model advertising and public relations. While at Honda, I was fortunate to make numerous trips to the factory in Japan where I tested pre-production bikes and worked directly with the engineers who designed each new bike. At that time, I was also part of an elite team of riders who set five FIM world speed records aboard the company's 1986 VFR750 street bike, one record being an average speed of 143 miles per hour for 24 hours. During the ten years I worked for two major motorcycle manufacturers, I tested, raced, and rode almost every type of motorcycle and ATV made, while my riding friends were following their racing careers.

In 1989, after four years with Honda, I discovered my entrepreneurial spirit and began working as a precision motorcycle rider and car driver for national television commercials and print advertising productions. My motorcycle industry work experience continued with brief stints as the aftermarket program director for the Motorcycle Industry Council (the motorcycle industry's trade association) for two years and as the marketing manager for the aftermarket performance company White Brothers for one year.

Even before I started MotoVentures in 1998, I had been teaching people how to ride most of my life. In fact, my teaching experience dates back to 1973, when at the age of 16 I began teaching others the trials riding skills that made me Arizona State Trials champion. Through the years, my competition experience has included various road races at Willow Springs Raceway and Laguna Seca Raceway, countless regional motocross races, numerous major desert races, including Barstow to Vegas and the Baja 1000, and many classic AMA National Enduros, including the Trask Mountain 2-Day Qualifier, the Quicksilver National, the Tecate 250, and even the Alligator Enduro in Florida.

Shortly after starting MotoVentures, I realized there was a definite need for higher-quality, more practical, real-world motorcycle rider training, so I immediately began developing my own curriculum and started writing this book. Today at MotoVentures, we continue to develop our teaching methods and curriculums as we offer motorcycle rider training for everyone from young beginner kids to military special forces men and everyone in between almost every week all year around at our private 350-acre Rider Training Center in southern California.

I have always had a true passion and enthusiasm for motorcycling and have dedicated my life to studying and practicing the art of riding motorcycles. I hope you enjoy reading *How to Ride Off-Road Motorcycles,* and I sincerely hope that you have a long and, above all, *safe* love affair with motorcycles too!

Introduction

To the uninitiated, riding an off-road motorcycle may look as easy as sitting down, putting your feet on the pegs, and twisting the throttle. But for any of us who have ever tried to tackle an off-road trail on a dirt bike, we know that there is so much more to the activity than that.

It is a widely acknowledged fact that off-road motorcycle riding (a.k.a., dirt-bike riding) is *the best way* to learn how to ride any kind of motorcycle, or take your riding to a higher level, and that proper rider training and practice is *the best investment* you can make to ensure a safe motorcycle riding future on, or off, the road.

Flying down a trail at speed on your off-road motorcycle is a freedom that very few people ever get to experience. Once you've tasted it, you'll find you can never get enough!

The book you are now holding is based on the curriculum of MotoVentures, a unique rider-training center in southern California that was founded in 1998. At MotoVentures, the staff uses off-road bikes to teach intensive motorcycle training curriculums that have been developed from more than 40 years of careful research and practice of all the techniques used by riders at the highest levels.

Who needs this book?

How to Ride Off-Road Motorcycles is a step-by-step practice guide written to help riders hone their off-road skills on their own. The book starts with basic exercises for someone's first ride and moves on to information for those who have attained expert status and can hang with the big dogs on a motocross track. The lessons and exercises in this book are the same ones that have been taught and practiced at MotoVentures since 1998. The book is written in frank laymen's terms, with practical real-world tips and advice that will help everyone from beginners who don't even know what "friction zone" means to experts who unfortunately know all too well what a "highside" is.

How to Ride Off-Road Motorcycles even covers specialized techniques that are used in motocross and trials competitions, representing the extreme opposite ends of the dirt-riding world. Even though it's obvious that this book was not written for street touring, cruising, or sport bike riders, they can certainly learn a few things by reading it, as well as becoming prepared if they ever get the opportunity to ride a dual-sport or dirt bike. *How to Ride Off-Road Motorcycles* was primarily written for dirt bike, dual-sport, motocross, and trials riders, adults and kids, beginners and experts— basically any performance-oriented motorcycle rider who wants to improve and take riding to the next level.

Benefits of reading
How to Ride Off-Road Motorcycles

This book will make you think about how you are riding now and offers specific ways you can practice and improve. For almost any motorcycle rider, reading this book will help reduce the chances of having an accident and the resulting injury or even death from riding. *How to Ride Off-Road Motorcycles* contains a lot of information and fundamentals in the first four chapters that you should understand and accept before moving on, including a full chapter on body positioning alone. From there, you'll find 14 chapters on a variety of riding exercises that are designed to help you practice and perfect these skills on your own. Each step-by-step exercise gets more challenging and includes advanced practice challenges. After the chapter on "power slides" come valuable chapters that cover important yet rarely discussed topics such as how to ride the variety of terrain you are likely to encounter, tips to practice good conduct and ride responsibly, how to prepare your bike, how specialized trials riding can dramatically improve your off-road riding skills, and how dirt riding can help your street riding skills. There is a glossary at the back of the book to help explain the many colorful terms used to describe off-road riding.

Good luck in your quest to become a better dirt bike rider.

1 New Rider Advice

There are plenty of things to learn

You've made the right choice. Off-road is the best place to learn to ride a motorcycle and it also happens to be a lot of fun. Unfortunately most people don't want to take the time to learn how to ride correctly and safely. They just want to ride as soon as possible. But to do it right, you must first learn how, just as if you were learning to drive a car or fly an airplane.

Riding a motorcycle is not rocket science, however. Most people can ride one with little or no instruction and ride for many years just barely getting by, but not safely. To ride a motorcycle correctly requires some good instruction and practice, practice, practice, which is what this book is all about.

Unfortunately, many people ride for many years before seeking instruction and by then may have already developed some bad habits, which can be tough to break. Especially in the beginning, good instruction is as important as wearing a full set of good riding gear. Beginners can be almost any age, and even if you're already riding street bikes or dual-sport bikes, it's never too late to learn and improve, and dirt-bike riding is just the ticket for that.

In this first chapter we'll talk about things like the earliest age kids can start riding, how to choose a dirt bike that will fit you best, and why protective off-road riding gear is one of the most important parts of dirt biking. We'll also identify what your dual-sport motorcycle options are, tips on finding a good used dirt bike, and choosing the right place to first learn and then practice at. Remember though, throughout this book our number-one objective is to ride safely and avoid accidents and injuries so you can enjoy off-roading for many years.

"There are so many great motorcycles, gear, and rider-training resources available today. One should be able to find a motorcycle for any budget, rider size, or ability. Test ride as many bikes as you can, and make sure you get well-fitting, safe riding gear. Cap that off with proper rider training and your off-road motorcycling experience should be extremely fun, safe, and rewarding."

Andy Leisner
Cycle World Magazine Publishing

Get good instruction

The first and best advice for new riders is to read this book and practice, practice, practice. If you really want to speed up the learning process, take a motorcycle rider training course taught by a professional. Chances are you took a lesson the first time you snow skied. For new riders, you will probably learn more in one day in a rider training course than you would in months, or even years, on your own, without forming bad habits. It is also not a good idea for self-taught people to teach others because they might pass along their own bad habits. On top of that is the reality that teaching someone you're close to, like a spouse or child, can generate unnecessary stress or friction. Reading this book or having a professional get you started right will be money well spent.

How old do you need to be to start riding off-road motorcycles?

Teenagers and adults can start riding motorcycles as long as they have the health, fitness, and physical abilities that riding requires. But we are often asked, "What is a good age to start a child riding a dirt bike?" Generally, we find that if a

kid can ride a bicycle well without training wheels, and really likes to ride bicycles, they may be ready for a dirt bike. You can buy training wheels for mini-bikes, but we believe kids should get their speed and balance figured out on a bicycle first so they don't need training wheels by the time they try out a mini-bike. Training wheels won't allow a bike to lean much, and this makes turning awkward. The child might as well be riding an ATV.

Speaking of ATVs, if you want your kids to eventually ride dirt bikes, avoid starting them on ATVs. They might develop bad habits and won't want to ride dirt bikes because they are considerably more challenging. Kids who can already ride two-wheelers can quickly learn to ride four-wheelers, but kids who only know how to ride ATVs may have difficulty adapting to dirt bikes. Of course, every kid matures differently, and just because a kid might be big enough doesn't mean he or she is mentally ready. Parents should remember that mini-bikes aren't babysitters. Young kids require a great deal of guidance, patience, and supervision. Really young kids sometimes have trouble concentrating and maintaining their focus. They have short attention spans and often lack the common sense (and healthy fear) we adults

Taking a moment to soak in the scene with your buddy is one of the best parts of a dirt bike adventure.

Knowing how to ride is only part of the equation. Having some mechanical ability, as well as planning ahead by packing the right tools and supplies, is all part of becoming a well-rounded off-road motorcyclist.

take for granted. Generally speaking, we find some kids are ready to try dirt-bike riding as young as four years old. For our very young students we use two great bikes from Yamaha, the PW50 and the TTR-50. These two little starter bikes have been the first bikes of many a champion rider.

What is the best bike for you?

Today's riders have many types of bikes available to them: street bikes, dual-sports, mini-bikes, off-road bikes, motocross bikes, trials bikes, and so on. In this chapter, we'll examine the options when it comes to picking a bike's physical size and engine size.

First (especially if you want to learn quickly), select a bike that you are not afraid to crash and possibly damage. Next, select a bike that is not too tall or has too much power so you can learn more at a faster rate. You can sit on different bikes at your local motorcycle dealership to see

how they fit and feel. If any of your pals has a dirt bike, you can try it out for a bit if they let you to see how you like that one. One of the best things a street-bike rider or dual-sport rider could do to improve his or her riding skills is to get a small, friendly off-road bike and take this book and go practice in the dirt for a while.

Your off-road motorcycle options range from mini-bikes for kids with engine sizes from 50cc to 125cc, on up to several adult size bikes with engine sizes from 250cc to 650cc. Your off-road motorcycle should feel comfortable while sitting or standing. You should feel confident and in control on it at any speed. For beginners, we recommend a dirt bike that is not too tall or it will be hard for to put their feet on the ground or one that is not too small or riders will feel cramped when riding it standing up. If you start riding at a young age you will outgrow your bike(s) and have to get a larger one. Shorter-than-average riders can make some changes such as modifying the suspension using lowering kits or cutting the seat foam to help reduce seat height. Taller-than-average riders can install taller handlebars or handlebar risers and a higher seat.

For the most part, wheel sizes and suspension travel determine how tall the seat will be. The distance from the seat to the footpegs may be the same on two different bikes, but if one bike has 10 inches of wheel travel (the distance the suspension moves when the bike hits a bump or lands from a jump), then the other bike with 12 inches of travel (which is standard on full-size bikes) will have a taller seat height. For height-challenged riders, if you can always keep your balance and keep your feet up, a tall bike is not a problem to ride. It's when you have to put your foot down to regain balance or stop that it's a problem. If you know how to ride, but you're not very tall, you can still ride a tall bike, you just have to learn to shift your butt completely off the seat to one side when coming to a stop so you can place only one foot on the ground at a time. Short riders tend to choose where they stop very carefully.

When it comes to choosing either a bike that fits now or one you can grow into, choose a bike that is friendly and appropriate for your height and skill level now so you can learn more quickly and ride to your bike's limits before moving up in size and power. Currently the major manufacturers offer roughly the following engine-sized recreational dirt bikes for kids of the following ages: 5- to 7-year-olds can ride a 50cc automatic clutch bike; 7- to 11-year-olds can ride a 90cc to 110cc automatic clutch bike. Motocross racing bikes are available for kids with 50cc, 80cc, and 125cc two-stroke engines and 150cc four-stroke engines.

And depending on their height, 12- to 16-year-olds can ride bikes with manual clutches with engine sizes from 125cc on up. People who are 5 feet, 6 inches to 5 feet, 8 inches will fit on bikes with 10-inch travel suspensions and moderate seat height. People taller than 5 feet, 8 inches can comfortably fit full-size off-road bikes with 12 inches of suspension travel and relatively tall seat heights.

Be sure to choose a bike with power you can handle. Today's off-road motorcycles are mostly four-strokes; the engine sizes of most off-road bikes range from as small as 50cc up to as large as 650cc. How much power a bike makes is less important in the beginning than how well it handles and suits you. More is not better when learning to ride a motorcycle; less is. Control is what you want so you can make the bike do what you're trying to learn.

A common dilemma for adults is whether to get a 250cc or a 450cc engine. Certainly if you're a big person, ride in high altitudes or soft, sandy, or muddy conditions, and like hillclimbing, the 450 is a better choice. Modern 250s perform so well they make a better choice for most people, who will find they can ride them faster and more confidently than a 450.

Racing bikes: two-stroke or four-stroke?

Back in the day, two-stroke–powered motorcycles were common, but not anymore. These days you can still purchase a two-stroke for recreational riding or racing, but it is becoming increasingly difficult for manufacturers to meet the stricter emission standards and two-strokes are being relegated primarily to racing only or discontinued altogether. Manufacturers must make bikes to meet the regulations of the day whether those regulations come from the government or a racing organization.

Other than the fact that the basic two-stroke engine design pollutes the environment more than a four-stroke, it makes great motorcycle engines and in some applications will be hard to replace. Two-stroke engines require mixing oil into the gas to lubricate the crankshaft and connection-rod bearings (a common ratio is 40:1, or 40 parts gas to 1 part oil, which is 16 ounces of oil to 5 gallons of fuel). Two-strokes have fewer moving parts so are therefore much lighter, have higher power-to-weight ratios, and are less expensive to produce, purchase, maintain, repair, and upgrade. Two-stroke engines rev quickly, have narrow power bands (the rpm range where the engine produces the strongest power), and minimal engine braking, and they don't like to idle for long without loading up. Quick-revving two-strokes are easy to kick-start (with a little throttle, please), require more use of the clutch, have hard-to-control wheelspin, and can more easily square off a turn and accelerate quickly. When climbing, two-strokes will continue to climb after shutting off the throttle. With a four-stroke, a rider must stay on the throttle until clearing the top. Because of its hyperactive nature, racing a two-stroke will wear you out quicker than racing a four-stroke.

Four-stroke engines are harder to kick-start, especially if you don't follow a precise procedure (usually with the right idle setting and no throttle required). Nearly all four-stroke recreational bikes come with electric starters and kick-starter back-ups. Four-stroke engines are more complex with more moving parts, making them inherently heavier. That complexity also makes them more time consuming and expensive to produce, purchase, maintain, repair, and

Tales from the Trail: MOTORCYCLE ENGINE EVOLUTION

In the late 1970s, the U.S. government toughened the emissions standards for street bikes, effectively ending the production and sales of two-stroke street bikes like the awesome Yamaha RD400. Of course, the four-strokes at the time were not up to the lighter weight and higher performance of the two-strokes of the day and all the purists were upset at the prospect of not being able to own a modern two-stroke street bike. Engineers got to work as they always do to close that performance gap. It took a few years, but they eventually produced four-stroke sport bikes that worked as well as the two-strokes. Today, the four-stroke sport bikes have such breathtaking performance that nobody misses two-stroke street bikes anymore. The same thing has happened with off-road bikes and the day will eventually come when we won't miss two-stroke off-road bikes either.

Going riding with veterans who know the terrain and the territory is always a good idea for newcomers to the sport.

upgrade. Four-strokes build revs (rpm) slower, have broader power bands, tend to get better traction in slippery conditions, and have a lot of engine braking (where the engine's compression slows you down when the throttle is shut off). When racing a four-stroke you can expect better traction on the starts, you will need to use the clutch less as the engine responds better to rolling on the throttle, and you can take wider lines where you can carry your momentum around a corner instead of the turn-and-burn method used for racing a two-stroke.

Engineers are now building four-strokes that outperform two-strokes, but it takes a bigger displacement four-stroke engine to make the same power of a two-stroke. (Generally speaking, it takes a 450cc four-stroke engine to equal the power of a 250cc two-stroke.) These great new four-strokes are more expensive than two-strokes, and the only way to make them lighter is to use more exotic metals, which will only drive up the price. In the future, consumers will just have to get used to higher weight standards and the higher costs that come with the price of performance without the pollution.

As dirt-bike designs have evolved and become more specialized, the differences between one model and another has grown. With so many kinds of bikes still available today the trick is to decide how and where you like to ride and carefully choose the right bike or "tool for the job" for you.

Do your research by talking to other riders, reading the enthusiast magazines, and talking to your dealer (just be careful, the dealer may be trying to clear his showroom floor of "just the right model for you").

Dual-sport motorcycle options: The 80/20 bike or the 20/80 bike

Dual-sport motorcycles are street legal but dirt capable to some degree. Dual-sport bikes were once called dual-purpose bikes and were once the largest segment of the motorcycle market. In the off-road market in America, dual-sport bikes represent approximately one-third of it, with off-road bikes and motocross bikes representing the other two-thirds. Dual-sports are usually owned and ridden by adults with street motorcycle operator endorsements on their licenses. They come in a wide variety of engine sizes, from 125cc to a whopping 1,200cc. By design, dual-sport bikes must work in two completely different worlds, on-road and off-road. Because of this, their performance must be compromised in either world. Dual-sport tires reflect this, and they still work amazingly well in both worlds. You can always mount up full-on street tires or dirt tires if you want.

Motorcycle manufacturers produce dual-sport bikes based on statistics that show how most dual-sport riders use their bikes, which is primarily on the street. Many factory dual-sport bikes are 80/20 bikes, meaning they are

80 percent street capable and 20 percent dirt capable. Fortunately you can also still purchase (or create) a 20/80 bike. If you don't have far to travel on roads to get to your preferred off-road riding areas, choose a 20/80 bike. If you primarily ride on the road and like to occasionally trek down dirt back roads, then choose an 80/20 bike. A popular new class of big dual-sport bikes is called Adventure Bikes and they require the skills in this book to ride well. But the real key to riding them successfully in the dirt is understanding the limitations of these large bikes and staying within them.

Finding a good used dirt bike

If you can't buy a new bike, you can buy a good used one if you know where to look and what to look for. The best way to buy a used bike is to buy a hand-me-down bike from someone you trust who knows what they're doing and will give you good advice and a maybe good deal too. Competition clubs are a good source for finding a used bike from an owner who is ready for a new bike and has one that is already set up for what you want to do. This is an

especially good way to find a used trials bike. If that doesn't work, you can look at what your local dealer might have taken in on trade and you can check the local newspaper for private party sales. These days we usually find what we're looking for in the local craigslist website or *Cycle Trader* website or magazine. When buying used, ideally you are looking for a bike with normal wear and tear by the original owner who loved the bike and is selling it for all the right reasons.

For clues about the bike's condition, start by assessing the owner. Did the owner use it for what it was designed? A good example is a recreational bike that was used for racing—it could be hammered. Ask how it was used, how often, and where they rode it. Ask if the engine and suspension are stock or modified. Ask if anything is broken or needs fixing. Ask about what maintenance or repairs have been performed and how often. Check the oil level and ask about oil and filter change intervals. Is the air filter clean? Look at the wear on the tires, chain, and sprockets. Will they need to be replaced soon? Spin the wheels; are they still round and

This rollercoaster sure looks like fun, doesn't it? Western riders are more used to wide open trails, while riders in the eastern half of the country typically ride in the woods.

Dirt biking is an E-ticket ride like no other. Not only is it thrilling and challenging, but an all-day ride will give anyone a great physical workout as well.

true or are they wobbling with dented rims? Check the skid-plate and undercarriage of the bike. Is it dented, scraped, and beaten up, which indicates riding over rocky terrain? Do the leading edges of the undercarriage look sandblasted? If so, it could have been used for high-speed sand or desert riding. How is the bike's overall condition? Was it kept in a garage or was it stored outside in the weather? And last, but not least, is it safe to ride? Do the brakes work? Does the throttle return and not hang up? Always be sure to check this on any bike you're about to ride. Finally, if you're not sure what to look for, bring a buddy who knows his way around a bike to help you out.

Electric-powered motorcycles

As enthusiasts we just want a bike that has great perfor-mance without sacrificing our environment. We really don't care how it is powered, as long as it rips. With that in mind, the bikes of tomorrow could be electric-powered. But don't hold your breath, they still have a long way to go before

equaling the incredible power that we are used to from a gas-powered bike. The electric bikes that are on the market now can't compare on most levels, and unfortunately, the cons still outweigh the pros. Stay tuned, though; many industry insiders agree that rapidly developing technology will make electric bikes a viable alternative someday. Until then, let's just enjoy to the fullest the bikes we have now.

Always wear a full set of protective riding gear

Don't be foolish, always dress for a crash—the cost of safety gear is cheap insurance. As with any sport, you will enjoy it even more if you have all the right equipment and gear that is available for that sport, and a full set of proper protective riding gear should be worn every time you ride a motorcycle.

A full set of off-road riding gear includes boots, heavy and tall socks, kneepads, heavy-duty pants, hip pads, heavy-duty jersey, elbow pads, shoulder pads, kidney belt, gloves (one pair for normal weather and one pair for cold weather),

The number of girls and women involved in the sport continues to grow every year. Don't ever let anyone tell you that dirt biking is for guys only!

By far the most important piece of safety equipment for dirt biking is the helmet. Today's skid lids are very lightweight, are affordable, and offer an incredible amount of protection.

a full-face helmet, goggles with different lenses for dark and light conditions and tear-offs or roll-offs for rain and mud conditions, a goggle-cleaning kit for long rides, a good jacket with a removable inner liner, and a large gear bag to carry it all in.

Off-road riding gear options and accessories include earplugs, a neck brace, knee braces, riding shorts, knee socks, hydration pack, backpack, fanny pack, thermal underwear, turtleneck sweater, jackets (one heavy for cold conditions and one light for mild weather), and a rain suit. Breathable Gore-Tex jackets are great since riding will make you sweat and that moisture must escape or you could get just as wet from your sweat as you would from not even wearing a jacket. Also, briefs are a better underwear choice for riding than boxers for what should be an obvious reason.

These days, you can purchase boots made specifically for motocross, recreational trail riding, ATVs, and even trials, and you can also purchase off-road riding gear made specifically for women, for dual-sport riding, motocross, off-road, and trials. Available are pants with pockets, pants that you don't have to tuck into your boots, and even riding pants with removable legs to form riding shorts. You can also get extra thick gear for the cold winters and extra vented gear for the hot summers. Most riders can get fully outfitted for as little as $500 or as much as $2,000 or more (used gear will save you a lot of dough, especially for kids). With all the great safety gear available today at affordable prices there's no excuse for not wearing it, and doing so will greatly reduce your risk of getting injured when you do crash.

Where to ride

It's important to choose the right location to take your first spin on a dirt bike and to practice the drills outlined for beginners in this book. The paved street in front of your house or a public motocross track are certainly *not* the best places to take your first ride, yet many have rolled their first wheels in even worse places. Of course, the street actually has too much traction and is usually surrounded with hard, unforgiving hazards, like cars and curbs, not to mention the fact that your dirt bike is not legal for the street.

To find where to ride locally, just ask another rider, visit your local bike shop, or contact the local or state land managers. There are basically four different kinds of riding areas: private property (with permission, of course), official public riding areas like on U.S. Forest Service or Bureau of Land Management land with a network of roads and trails, racetracks, as well as a whole lot of "gray areas" that are usually unmaintained private property that may or may not be closed the next time you go there. Public riding areas can be found on most maps. Be sure to get the latest map from that area's land manager office.

Try to find a place that's not too congested or distracting, not too sandy or too muddy, and a place with a variety of gentle terrain challenges. Motocross tracks are usually too crowded and present too many tough challenges right off the bat. The ideal place is a large flat, firm dirt field, devoid of trees, rocks, and other obstacles to run into. After choosing a good place, identify the area hazards with everyone and set boundaries of where everyone should and shouldn't go. Always supervise new riders and keep them in sight. Take time to advise young riders of common rules of the road that adults take for granted, like always stay to the right on *all* blind turns and rises. Beginners need space to fumble around at first and figure it all out. Once you have the basics down, travel a little and try other places to ride. You might be surprised how fun the riding is around you and the experience on different terrain or tracks will make you a better rider.

Find a riding partner

You'll need at least one good riding partner, preferably someone who is better or more knowledgeable than you so you can learn from that person. Pick your riding partners carefully, and if you don't know anyone to ride with it is relatively easy to find someone, especially with today's social media and instant internet searches and communications. Go to a popular riding area "On Any Sunday" (and check out the 1971 documentary with that title) and you will meet plenty of people who will probably let you ride with them. Motorcycle shops are also good sources to find riding partners. Regional enthusiast publications post schedules of local races, rallies, tours, fundraisers, poker runs, and more. You can also meet a lot of people by attending local races, joining a local riding club, or entering an organized local ride.

What to do before and after riding

Preparation is the key to any successful ride. Any time you go riding it is important to check to make sure everything's working correctly on your bike. If you have any questions about how to maintain your bike, all the basic information is in your bike's owner's manual and almost everything you need to know about your bike can be found in your bike's service manual.

Before you start any bike, check the brakes and also make sure the throttle returns or fully closes when twisted and released. Turn the handlebars and try the throttle—does it still snap closed when released? Do the clutch and shift levers function properly? Is there gas in the tank and oil in the engine? Is the gas petcock on? Is the air filter clean? Is the chain lubed and adjusted properly? Is the battery charged? Do the lights work? Are there any loose nuts, bolts, or screws? Does the bike roll freely, or did you accidentally bend a brake rotor on the last ride and are finally noticing it just before going on the next ride?

Tires and pressures: Remember, your two little motorcycle tire contact patches are your only connection with earth so the condition of your tires and the pressures of the inner tubes inside the tires are critical to riding safely and correctly. For off-roaders, there's nothing better than fresh knobby tires, but unfortunately they don't last long in some terrains. Tire wear is expected, of course, and will increase with the abrasiveness of the terrain you're riding in, like rocks. Riding on pavement will really ruin a good knobby in a short time. But tires are designed to wear out if they're doing a good job, and considering their importance, it would be wise (and cheap insurance) to always use good tires.

Correct tire pressures are critical on any motorcycle and should be checked before every ride. Off-road bike tires can get small thorns, a loose valve stem, or just slowly leak between rides. The correct tire pressures will vary, depending on the bike and tire being used and on the speeds and terrain you are riding in. You can run higher tire pressures and avoid flats and dented wheel rims but have reduced traction and feel. You can run lower tire pressures and risk flats and wheel dents, but enjoy better traction and feel. It's a compromise and something you can experiment with (as well as ask of other riders who have experience in that type of terrain).

Tales from the Trail:
DON'T JUDGE A BIKE BY ITS BODY

My first bike was a used 1966 Hodaka Ace 90, and it looked to me just like a real full-size, big boy's bike. One day, while riding out in the desert, I came across a guy on a Vespa. Thinking I was on a real bike and he was just on a scooter, I challenged him to a race. To my surprise, he soundly beat me. I didn't even think about what size engine he had in it. As it turned out, he had a 250cc engine against my 90cc engine. Now I always make sure I pick races with bikes my own size regardless of what they look like.

Note: Generally, street bike tires are tubeless. Inner tubes are primarily a dirt bike, off-road, and dual-sport bike thing where tires must flex a lot and flats are more common.

People who drive for hours to get to a riding area and after unloading their bikes discover they aren't even ready to ride always surprise us. Experienced riders will check their bikes thoroughly before every ride, especially on a bike they don't already know. See Chapter 20 for some tips on tuning, maintaining, and upgrading your bike.

Prepare your transporter and support equipment. Is your transporter ready? If it's going to be a long, tough ride, the last thing you want to deal with is transporter problems. Tie your bikes down securely so they don't fly out or cause damage to your bike or transporter if you hit a bump in the road. You can use fork spring savers like braces and wheel chocks and a good cable lock if carried in an open pick-up or trailer. It's also a good idea to leave your transporter keys in a secret place on the transporter so that someone else could get it for you if need be. Of course, you'll need to pack certain support equipment in your transporter like extra gas in cans (Note: Don't fill gas cans in the bed of your truck or risk ignition from static electricity. Take them out and fill them while they are sitting on the ground), a bike stand, air pump, and tools. Certain replacement or spare parts are good to pack, too, so something minor like a broken clutch lever doesn't ruin your entire trip. Last, pack plenty of food and water because off-road riding will make you hungry and thirsty.

These completely different tire treads reflect the requirements for each terrain they're used on, from left to right; street tire, dual sport tire (dirt or street), trials tire (rocky terrain), knobby tire (for off-road or motocross), and paddle tire (for sand dunes).

Prepare for the riding area requirements. Different riding areas have different requirements. Make sure you know the rules and regulations of each area before you go. A few good examples are: You must have a whip antenna if riding at the sand dunes, a spark arrestor and the correct state registration if riding on most public lands (in California you'll also need an Adventure Pass). More and more areas also have sound restrictions now as well. Some areas have open staging areas and some are restricted to only certain spots. Most public riding areas are managed and have trails and routes that are marked and maintained. This means they could be closed for various reasons and could wreck your plans to ride there. It's a good idea to check with the land managers of that area and pick up the latest maps before beginning your trip.

Prepare your body, riding gear, and what you carry when riding. Get a good night's sleep the night before your ride, be sure to hydrate with water, eat a good breakfast, and warm up and stretch out your muscles just before taking off. A good diet can make or break a ride. Before a ride, avoid eating foods that upset your stomach, such as onions and nuts. The extreme motions combined with stomach gas can make you sick.

As veteran riders will tell you, *always dress for the crash* by wearing a full set of riding gear from head to toe. Decide what to carry on you and how to carry it. Some items can be carried on the bike and some items should be carried on you, especially emergency items such as your cell phone, water, a first aid kit, and a Spot Locator (emergency GPS locator). You'll need certain tools, the bike's registration, and a map. To carry it all, you can use a backpack or a fanny pack. If riding with friends you can split it up between everyone. If you don't want to carry everything yourself, just make sure you invite along an ex–Boy Scout buddy who will carry it all for you.

Keep in mind that everything you carry, either on your bike or body, has to be extra secure. The jarring you will be taking on a ride is incredible and will shake anything loose that isn't tied down correctly.

All off-road riders should be prepared for a crash or mechanical issue that could leave them stranded. What if you or someone you're with gets a flat tire? What if your engine quits or runs out of gas? What if your chain breaks? You can't call for someone to come get you unless you have a satellite phone, and even if you could call, you might be in a place so remote a truck can't get there. You will have to either repair it on the spot or get a tow from another bike. For flats, make

Dirt bikes come in a wide variety of physical sizes and engine sizes to fit everyone from young kids to adults. Here are some recent Yamaha offerings for recreational dirt bikes, from left to right; PW50, TTR50, TTR90, TTR125, TTR125L, TTR230, WR250, and WR450.

sure you carry everything you'll need: a 21-inch spare inner tube that can be used in the 18- or 19-inch rear tire too. Carry air (we use CO2 cartridges and an applicator). You'll need tools to pull the wheels off the bike and "tire irons" to take the tires off the wheel rims to get to the tubes. We recommend practicing fixing a flat first in your garage so you can test your tools and techniques in a relaxed and clean environment. If your bike's engine won't run or maybe your drive chain is busted, you can be towed by someone if you carry a towrope. As a last resort, you can manually push someone, but this is both difficult and dangerous. For more on towing and pushing see Chapter 7, which addresses hillclimb extractions and bump starting.

What to do after a day of riding: You're tired and facing a long trip home. You must first pack up camp and securely load your bikes. (Don't leave any litter! That's one of the things that closes down riding areas.) After arriving home, if you're not too tired, try to unload everything and wash both your bike and your riding gear as soon as possible (the next day at the latest). If you can, put your bike on a bike stand so you can relax the suspension and spin both wheels, especially the rear. To wash your bike, first get it wet, rinse it off, and then use a product like Simple Green to help wash off the dirt and grease. Be careful about where

you direct your water pressure so you don't force water where it shouldn't be, like down the exhaust pipe (plugs are available) or into the suspension pivots. A mud scraper can be handy for clearing under fenders after really muddy days. After washing, towel dry your plastic to avoid water spots and use good old WD-40 on all the joints, pivot points, bare metal surfaces, and the chain to make sure there's no water remaining there. Trivia note: WD-40 stands for the 40th water-displacement formula the company tried that really worked.

After washing, you should start the engine and let it warm up and dry out. Once it's clean you can inspect your bike for worn or broken parts so you can repair or replace them in time for the next ride. Unless the bike needs additional maintenance or repairs, checking the gas and oil, adjusting and lubing the chain, cleaning the air filter, and checking the tire air pressures should be all you need to do.

Finally, look at your equipment and riding gear. Open your gear bag and let everything dry out. Wash what needs washing and inspect all riding gear for wear and damage so it can be repaired or replaced before the next time you want to ride. Waiting until the last minute to prepare for a ride is asking for easily avoidable problems that can ruin your whole ride.

2 Beginners' First Steps

How to make this critical time a fun learning experience

If you already know the basics of riding, do you remember the first time you tried to ride, the first time you rolled a wheel, let out the clutch, and gassed it? And how was that first stopping experience for you? Chances are nobody helped you because they didn't know what to say or how to teach it. Chances are you made all the mistakes and maybe even crashed a time or two. It doesn't have to be that way anymore. If you've never ridden off-road at all, you'll need to follow this chapter as if you were the student. On the other hand, you will probably someday soon be in a position to teach a first-timer, and in that case put yourself in the role of the teacher in this next chapter.

Remember, whenever you are teaching or practicing with young kids, supervise them at all times. Kids need specific directions and, even better, an adult rider they can follow at first who

"I prefer to teach people how to ride on the dirt versus any other type of terrain. In the right environment, it can provide a safe and relatively stress-free way to understand throttle and clutch control along with shifting and braking techniques. I typically start by having new riders do figure 8s in a pattern that is approximately 75 yards deep. This allows people to gain muscle memory for all the necessary control inputs and learn body position for both left- and right-hand turns. As they learn, they can introduce more speed in the straightaway and then try to tighten up the turns."

Ken Faught
Former Dirt Rider Magazine *editor-in-chief, former* Cycle News *associate editor, co-founder of Pole Position Raceway, three-time motorcycle land-speed record holder, former I.S.D.E. competitor, former Team Makita Suzuki MX PR coordinator*

For a beginner, having a good coach will really speed up the learning process. The best coaching usually involves explaining the exercise, demonstrating the exercise, then observing and adjusting as the student rides the exercise over and over.

knows where to go and where not to go. For example, young kids don't know to stay to the right around blind corners and to stay out of high-traffic areas.

Begin by holding a "riders meeting." Instructors should tell students what they will be doing that day and what they expect from them. You can also take this time to give them a quick overview about safety precautions, rules of conduct, responsibilities and riding etiquette, the importance of a full set of riding gear, riding area requirements and familiarization, environmental concerns, visual and mental habits, and body positioning.

Next, introduce the bike they will be riding. Walk around it and identify everything, point out all the controls and demonstrate how to use them with the engine off. Have them try them all without the engine running. Describe the importance of good clutch control. Explain the friction zone (the point where the bike begins to move while releasing the clutch). Explain the shift pattern. Instruct them to kick up the side stand before mounting the bike and to keep it up when dismounting the bike. This is necessary because your weight will make the long travel suspension move so much you won't be able to use the side stand while sitting on the bike. Show them how to stabilize the bike and keep it from rolling when mounting and dismounting by holding the front brake on (with two fingers, of course).

Next, have them try all the controls on the bike and dry shift the transmission with the engine off. For dry shifting, it helps to rock the bike forward and rearward without the clutch to help the transmission change gears. Demonstrate

proper body positions. Tell them where to place their feet. Have them mount and dismount on both sides. Have them walk alongside and push their bike a short distance to get a feel for its weight and balance. Point out how easy a bike is to control at no or low speed when it is kept perpendicular to the ground.

Finally, show them how to start up the engine and how to shut it off too. If the engine is cold, show them how to use the carburetor choke. Now, with full gear on, let them sit on the running bike, twist the throttle, and feel the engine's rpm rise and fall. One of the last things you can tell them before the next step is "put your brain in gear before you put the bike in gear."

Kick-starting a bike is becoming a lost art as many four-strokes now feature electric starters. To kick-start a bike you must move the kick lever quickly with your leg until it stops against the footpeg. If you're not tall enough, or strong enough, or the bike has a lot of compression, you may need to jump in the air with your left leg so you can come down hard on the kick lever with your weight and leg. It also helps to place your left leg higher on a stand, log, or rock, to place you above the kick lever. To kick-start a four-stroke it helps if you start on the compression stroke and make sure the idle is correct so you won't need to give it any throttle. To kick-start a two-stroke that is already warmed up, it helps to give it the throttle a little twist just when your foot meets the footpeg when the engine's piston is moving up and down the quickest.

With some students you may only need to demonstrate what you want them to do. The problem is you better make sure you're demonstrating correctly or you could be passing along your bad habits.

Note: Most off-road motorcycles can start in gear with the clutch pulled in, but many off-road motorcycle engines have maladjusted or worn-out manual clutches that don't fully disengage and drag the engine down when trying to start in gear with the clutch in. Of course the solution to this is to fix your clutch, or, like many riders do, simply put up with it and make sure to always start your bike in neutral.

Stop-and-go practice

The first thing beginners must demonstrate while riding is their ability to start moving and come to a stop smoothly. With the engine warmed up and running in neutral, make sure they straighten the handlebars and have a clear path forward. Have them sit forward on the seat, as well as lean a little forward, too, with their arms bent (a typical beginner mistake is having their arms too straight while sitting rearward on the bike). Instructors should stand a little off to the side in front of the student.

Note: Many small dirt bikes have three-speed transmissions with automatic clutches instead of a manual clutch, so small, young riders (four to nine years old) do not have to release a clutch lever to start moving, they just have to put it in gear (at idle!) and gently twist the throttle. Many small dirt bikes come with adjustable screws to limit the throttle opening so parents can control the bike's top speed during the learning phases.

After putting the bike in first gear, have your students place both feet on the ground. It's important for beginners to feel secure at this point. Instruct them to slowly (and partially) release the clutch while giving it a little throttle so they can feel the "friction zone" where the bike begins to move forward. After they creep a short distance with both feet out (acting like a centipede), have them pull the clutch in and stop. Repeat this several times while increasing the distance they ride each time.

To stop during this first exercise, tell new riders to primarily use (apply) their rear brake at first, but instruct and encourage them to gradually start using the front brake at the same time, using just two fingers and the correct handgrip, of course.

Next, tell them to keep their feet out when they start rolling. When they pick up a little speed, they can pick up their feet and place them on the footpegs. Now they can ride along in first gear getting a feel for gentle throttle acceleration and deceleration. Have them repeat this stop-and-go process many times until they are comfortable

Tales from the Trail:
MY FIRST RIDE AND CRASH

I got my first bike (Hodaka Ace 90) and immediately started riding it in our backyard in the suburbs. My family did their best to explain how to ride it, but most of what they said went in one ear and out the other. When it came time for me to actually take my first ride, my two older brothers jumped in to help. So with me on board and the bike running, one brother held the throttle while the other jammed it in gear. I never got a chance to even use the clutch. I took off and was riding somewhat under control for about 50 feet until I ran out of backyard and had to turn around. I didn't even know how to slow down, much less how to turn around, so I ran directly into the chain-link fence that separated us from our neighbors. I bent the fence for my dad to fix and put the first scratches on both myself and my new bike. My brothers got a good laugh out of it. I was just happy to finally be riding. My firsthand experience of how *not* to start out is why I started training beginners and wrote this book, so others can have a more positive first riding experience than I did.

with coordinating the clutch and throttle. *Do not* allow any new rider to dump the clutch or release it too rapidly, which they can get away with on a little bike. Point out how good clutch control is critical to ride in the hills and to ride bikes with more horsepower. To help a rider who wants to release the clutch too rapidly, try tossing a rock about 20 feet in front of the new rider and instruct the rider to not fully release the clutch until he or she picks up a little speed and gets to that rock. New riders can dump their clutch later, long after they first demonstrate their ability to release it slowly.

Of course, during this critical stop-and-go practice they are all learning throttle control and coordinating the throttle with the clutch and gaining confidence with every move. Remind them that the clutch is the first thing they must do before putting the bike in gear to go somewhere and the clutch is also the first thing they must do before they stop somewhere. If they master the clutch, they will be able (eventually) to ride almost any motorcycle.

First turning practice

In order for beginners to continue learning how to shift and speed up and slow down in a controlled setting where a coach can stand nearby, we suggest laying out a slightly tighter course, maybe even use just two corners like an oval race track. This way they can start learning how to turn while practicing everything else. Have them ride around sitting down and turn to the left first, then switch to practice turning right. A simple figure 8 course is a lot of fun as well.

Instruct them to use both brakes lightly, turn tight to the right and to the left in first gear, and shift up and down on the straights. For more detailed instructions on how to practice sitting turns, see Chapter 6.

After beginners conquer starting and stopping, shifting, and the first turning exercises, they can move on to practice the rest of the exercises outlined in this book, which includes braking, stand-up riding, stand-up turning, uphills, downhills, side hills, turns on

Releasing the Clutch

1 To teach a beginner how to release the clutch and begin riding, first tell them what you want them to do, especially the importance of sitting forward on the seat and leaning forward when feeling for the clutch's friction zone for the first time.

2 Teachers can stand a few feet ahead, but not directly in front, and the rider should just creep a few feet at a time before pulling in the clutch and stopping again.

3 Until they acquire a feel for the friction zone and are able to pick up a little speed they can keep their feet out and "Centipede," or move their feet alternately on the ground as they move forward.

Release and Roll

1 Releasing the clutch and rolling for the first time is easy if you follow this step-by-step process. Start by sitting forward on the seat.

2 Put the bike in first gear and place both feet on the ground. Lean forward and slowly, but only partially, release the clutch lever.

3 As the bike reaches the friction zone and begins to move forward, make sure to move your feet, keep the bike perpendicular to the ground, and try to keep the handlebars straight.

hills, and how to get unstuck from hills. From there, beginners will progress at different rates and can continue training with the help of the remainder of exercises in this book. Now go out and have fun practicing.

Shifting practice

Once a new rider is able to start and stop, their next step is learning how to shift. Explain the shift pattern on the bike they are riding before they mount the bike and start the engine. The standard gear shift pattern on most motorcycles is one down and five up, meaning first gear is one shift down from neutral and second through sixth are one shift up at a time. Neutral is a "half-click" or half of a full shift lever movement between first and second gear. The easiest way to find neutral is to shift down to first gear and then move the lever a half click upward.

After just a few fundamental exercises. new riders might be ready for a fun, easy trail ride, but leaders should only take them on pre-scouted skill-building routes like this one at our training center. Remember, you can take a good ride and stay together if the leader doesn't run off and always stops at major cross-roads and the last rider, or sweep rider, never passes anyone!

One of the very first things to practice is gently stopping with the rear brake and front brake, concentrating on the fundamentals. Use two fingers only on the front brake, squeeze the brake lever progressively, keep your bike perpendicular to the ground, with your wheels in line, and your handlebars straight. Remember, this is just the beginning of braking practice and should continue until you fear no downhill.

Tales from the Trail:
RIDING LIKE A FISH OUT OF WATER

I went to work for Kawasaki Research and Development as a test rider and mechanic at just 20 years old, so needless to say my fitness and motorcycle-riding skills were good at the time. My new friends there decided to take me jet skiing and, of course, told me nothing about how to do it. On top of that, we went to the Pacific Ocean—hardly the best place to go for the first time. I thought it would be easy, but spent the entire day crashing and trying to keep up. I rode like a fish out of water. Of course my friends were brutal and ran circles around me while I floundered. That night I thought about it a lot and figured it out. The next day I went out again and was immediately able to ride, and after only half the day was almost keeping up. From this experience I now reserve judgment on new riders knowing that with a little time they too will probably figure it out.

Point out that you shift only one gear at a time and then move your foot away from the shift lever. Remind them to be sure they shut the throttle off every time they shift and advise them to not look down to shift or use the rear brake. In addition, once they get a feel for their engine's sound and feel when accelerating and decelerating at various speeds, they will know when to shift or not and it will become unnecessary to count their gear shifts. Downshifting is usually performed while slowing down, or they can stop in any gear. They just can't take off again until they shift the bike back down into a lower gear, at least second, and preferably first.

To practice shifting, have them ride around a large square or rectangular area with 90-degree slow corners and relatively long straightaway (follow our "First Turning Practice" instructions previously mentioned). Ask them to ride around, and while they do, listen to their engine's rpm to make sure they are shifting at the right places and times. If they are revving their engine too much, point out that they can shift early (short shift) before optimum rpm, which will make their acceleration (and deceleration) not so abrupt. Caution them that if they downshift more than one gear before slowing their speed enough, too much high engine braking could make the rear tire momentarily lock up.

When new riders get to this exercise they are able to ride around safely and are now able to start combining exercises such as clutching, shifting, and braking. In a later chapter they can take what they know now and learn the next big step, which is turning.

In some exercises like this hillside extraction your instructor should remain nearby to help if you lose your balance. To practice this exercise, simply stall the bike in gear on a medium-size uphill, dismount and lean your bike into your hip, pull in your clutch and roll backward and around until pointing slightly downhill, and as you go back down control your speed with the front brake. Remember to always maintain your balance with one foot uphill whenever remounting and starting to roll downhill.

3 Foundation Building

It is important to understand the fundamentals of how all motorcycles stop and turn in order to ride them well

At MotoVentures we teach control, help build confidence and form good habits, and create safe riders for life. We believe you wouldn't try to develop good riding skills based on bad fundamentals any more than you would build a good house on a bad foundation. It is a lot easier to create good habits at first than it is to suffer from bad ones for years and eventually have to correct them. Once you've learned how to ride correctly, take the time to practice and it will pay off, because with motorcycling, the higher-skilled riders simply have more fun. Riding a motorcycle is like playing an instrument or riding a bicycle; you may be able to pick it up after some time off, but you'll be rusty and it'll be hard to get back to your old skill level. The lesson here is, better use it, or you could lose it.

Good riders didn't get that way overnight; it took years. If you start at a young age, you can learn quickly because you are both fearless and durable. You can make mistakes, dust yourself off, and try again. Today's young riders expect to become good quickly, like they can

"When riding at high speeds, you always want to pan out and back with your eyes—things can happen real fast the faster you ride. A lot of riders never look out far enough, which gets them in trouble. Another thing is, when I go riding with guys, I notice in the more technical areas they don't carry enough momentum and end up with a stupid tip-over crash. Always carry enough momentum to keep you moving. Do whatever it takes to get over the obstacle, and then you can pull yourself back into shape after the obstacle."

Ty Davis
AMA Supercross champion, AMA National Enduro champion, ISDE Gold Medalist, WORCS Series champion, Baja 500 and Baja 1000 (four-time) winner, voted "Best All-Around Rider" by Dirt Rider Magazine *three years in a row*

with computer games, but in the real and consequential world of motorcycle riding, you can't become an expert overnight. If you start at an older age, it is essential that you try to avoid making mistakes and always ride correctly. Learning to ride can be frustrating for some who completely understand what to do, and maybe even do it correctly occasionally, but struggle getting their bodies to do what their minds want them to do. There's no way around it, good riding habits take time to develop no matter how old you are. The best way to speed up the process is to take this book and go practice often.

In this chapter, we review how practicing and perfecting key fundamental skills will improve your control, confidence, and safety, and take your riding to the next level. We discuss what qualities good riders possess and the importance of having good mental habits, visual habits, and practice ethics. We discuss how speed is just a tool you can use where needed, and we even point out what to expect if you crash.

Note: After you conquer the basics and continue to practice, don't be afraid to try other bikes. By test riding other bikes you will learn how your bike's performance compares to them. Maybe you'll discover that you need to tune up your bike or maybe it's time to get another bike

now that you know what you're missing. These days you have many different, incredibly good bikes out there to choose from.

Are you just good enough to be dangerous?

There's a point where a rider gets beyond the beginner jitters and becomes overconfident and will try things he or she is not actually ready for. There are signs everyone should be aware of so we can identify this dangerous condition and correct it before they have an accident. Just because someone is an experienced rider doesn't necessarily mean they are good rider. We've seen many people with years of experience who were terrible riders. People who are impatient, overly confident, and have inflated egos often discover too late the consequences of riding a motorcycle badly. Typically, they overestimate their abilities and underestimate the danger. Some are naturally coordinated and can pull it off, while others who are not suffer the consequences.

Maybe you know someone or maybe it's you, but you have to ask: When you ride do you scare yourself and others? Are you making it up as you go, winging it, and really don't know what you're doing? Has your riding ever

When riding slowly and turning you must turn the handlebars and counterbalance to keep from falling over.

When turning at mid to high speeds you will no longer need to turn the handlebars, simply lean your bike, but you must still counterbalance a little.

been described as sketchy? Do you crash on every ride? Are you always the last rider back to the truck and do you always have a "how I cheated death" story to tell? If you or someone you know fits this description, you may be just good enough to be dangerous, and if you or your friend doesn't receive proper training and practice immediately, it could mean a rough or maybe abbreviated motorcycle-riding future.

Fear factor

It's normal for new riders to experience emotions like fear, anxiety, and inhibition when attempting a challenging new activity like riding a motorcycle. Everyone learns and progresses at a different rate and some take longer than others. Everyone has to overcome one or more of these emotions when they start and the best way is with slow, steady progression by building their control and confidence in an ideally suited riding area (not too sandy, rocky, hilly, and so on) and on a bike that fits them and is not too big or powerful. You can't be fearful and ride well, but you do need to have a healthy respect for it, allow yourself enough time to learn at your own pace, and develop the control and confidence that riding requires, and you can conquer those natural emotions.

Think in terms of how you can help your motorcycle

Like any serious endeavor, motorcycling requires many things, starting with the right attitude. You've got to want it, and you've got to pay attention to all the details. Instructing someone who is there for the wrong reasons can be a real challenge. Examples include when a kid rides because their dad wants it but they don't (it happens), when someone is riding just to impress a boyfriend or girlfriend, when someone is riding just to hang with the boss. These are all dangerous reasons for riding. Motorcycle riding demands your full attention *and* efforts. *You must take it very seriously because complacency leads to crashing.*

Some common qualities of good riders are hard to teach, but in some cases can be developed. Coordination is important. You must be able to control your body to make it do what you want it to do. We've seen people who fully understand what to do, but can't make their bodies do it. Common sense is important too. You must use good judgment constantly when riding a motorcycle, and it helps to have good instincts. Some examples of bad riding judgment might include not accelerating before sand, not slowing down before a turn, riding in blinding dust, or picking a bad line. There are plenty of examples. One of the most

When riding briskly you can also turn your bike by brake sliding or power sliding and are able to lean with the bike.

This is an incorrect upper body position for standing turns. This rider's shoulders and torso are crossed up or twisted, and his outside knee is also pressed against the bike, which hinders counterbalancing. In both sitting and standing turns, if you can't make tight turns and are constantly running wide on turn exits, you're probably riding all crossed up like this.

Dirt bike riding is challenging and you will be taking some spills. Fortunately, the overwhelming majority of accidents result in little injury to either rider or bike.

important qualities you must have is respect. You can't be afraid of riding, but you need a healthy respect for it and should always stay within your limits. If you are fearless, you better be really good because fearless motorcycle riders usually don't last long.

A great way to prepare for your first dirt bike lessons is to put plenty of time on bicycles, preferably mountain bikes. Any bicycle riding will help prepare you physically and mentally for riding motorcycles. Mountain bike riders who take up motorcycle riding immediately know how to pick a line to follow. Note: If you ride both mountain bikes and motorcycles I recommend that you move the front brake lever to the right side like it is on motorcycles, making your bicycle an even better training tool for riding your

motorcycle. (You had better let anyone know that the switch has been made if they happen to hop on your bike, though!)

One of the beauties of motorcycling is that it is different for everyone. You can ride fast or slow, go left or right, up or down, or you can become a professional racer or a casual recreation rider. It's the ultimate freedom machine. Good riders get that way because they love to ride and practice often. They embrace challenges and want to learn more, are rarely satisfied, and always seek perfection. Good riders have developed incredible feel and become one with their bikes with it becoming an extension of their body. Good riders use less physical energy and fuel, create less wear, and tend not to crash and damage their bikes, all while still riding faster than most other people.

Expert riders can immediately spot a good rider from a not-so-good rider, especially after riding just a few minutes together. One sign of a nervous novice would be dangling both legs on the ground when coming to a stop or rounding a slow turn. Unless you want to project to everyone that you are a rookie, when stopping, try to just put one foot down and don't ever put your outside leg out in a turn.

You don't necessarily need great balance to ride motorcycles well, but you do have to seek balance. You can't argue with the laws of gravity. Simply put: *Motorcycles are inherently unstable and will fall right over if you let them.* At rest, have you ever noticed how easy it is to handle a motorcycle of any size when you keep it absolutely perpendicular to the ground? It's only when you lean them that you feel their weight and they want to fall over. You must constantly work at keeping your balance to ride motorcycles well. Note: When you start riding, you may develop sore "motorcycle muscles" and even blisters and eventually calluses on your hands.

Tales from the Trail:
THEIR LAST GUESS IS TRAINING

Let's face it, riding a motorcycle isn't hard, but riding one correctly (safely) is. There are many people who have been riding for many years but are still not skilled at it. At some point they get fed up with being the last rider back or always crashing, and they finally come to us for some training. After correcting numerous bad habits they have acquired over the years and teaching them the right way to ride and practice, we encourage them to practice even more before going riding with their buddies again. When they finally do, they find themselves riding up front and not crashing all day. The funny thing is their buddies first suspect it is because they have been working out or maybe they tuned up their bike, when the real reason is they are finally riding correctly.

If you keep a bike absolutely perpendicular to the ground it takes very little effort to hold it up.

If you lean a bike at low speeds, or no speed, it becomes heavy and very difficult to hold up!

Confidence is the key. You must have confidence to ride well and the only way to get it is by practicing and training. Confidence is common among all motorcycle racers. They must fully believe in themselves and cannot doubt or hesitate or they will either crash or lose. When you talk to a motorcycle racer they can seem arrogant to those who don't understand what it takes to do what they do. Confidence is a major factor in their ultimate success or failure.

Mental and visual habits: no surprises

Good riding requires good mental habits, good visual habits, and even good hearing and sense of smell too. Good riders rely on almost every sense they have to help them quickly identify and correctly respond to a variety of situations and conditions they may encounter.

Mentally, you should prepare by reading this book and by practicing "perfectly" so that when the time comes and you need to react in a split second for an emergency riding situation you won't have to think about it and will respond correctly. Practicing leads to confidence, which makes you both mentally and physically prepared. If you are not prepared, you may doubt or hesitate, and avoid attacking a hillclimb or not be aggressive enough in a sand wash. When riding off-road, there are many situations where you will be better off going for it than being tentative.

Visually, you must constantly scan far ahead, as well as just in front. Make sure you focus on the path you want to follow and not "target-fixate" on any hazard, or you may just end up hitting it. As your speed increases you must look farther ahead, but you can't ignore something in the foreground either. It's your number-one job to identify everything and not let anything surprise you or sneak up on you. Simply put, if you can't see something or don't know how to ride the terrain, slow down or stop altogether.

Audibly, you must listen to the different sounds your bike makes. Take note of how it sounds and accelerates at different rpm and in different gears so you can adjust your gear selection or throttle position for either more smooth operation or for maximum performance. Of course, with anything mechanical you must always listen for anything unusual. Many times hearing and even smelling changes in an engine have helped a racer save an engine from blowing up. If you are used to how your bike sounds when it's running well, you will be able to recognize when it's not and do something about it before it gets worse.

The checklist

We recommend the following mental checklist to go through as you approach challenging sections: (1) Read the terrain; (2) select the best line to take; and (3) execute by using the correct techniques. Note: As you become more skilled and experienced, this checklist will become automatic with your brain processing all this information instantly.

1. Terrain reading: Take terrain reading seriously and you won't be surprised by it. Terrain reading means to have the ability as you ride to identify and adapt to the wide variety of surfaces and obstacles on those surfaces. For street riders, that means watching out for water, spilled gas, sand and gravel, slick painted lines, and more on the road. If you're going to ride a motorcycle in a diverse environment like off-road or dual-sport, you had better develop good visual habits and get good at reading all kinds of terrain. Is the terrain you're approaching hard or soft? Is it smooth or bumpy? Is there any traction or not? Good riders can read terrain (and its geography and topography) quickly as they approach at speed, while new riders would be better off slowing or stopping before the hazard and assessing the challenge before proceeding. This is where many mistakes are first made: by failing to identify hazardous terrain and respond appropriately. Master terrain reading and you'll never be surprised because you didn't identify the hazards. A lot of that learning simply comes with experience.

2. Line selection: Pick and stick to the smoothest, highest-traction line you can. In the motorcycle world, "the line" is a specific narrow path you want your tires to follow. Keep in mind that when turning at slow speed your rear tire will track inside the radius of the front tire, so make sure to leave room for it on the inside. Once you've read the terrain correctly it's time to pick a specific line that offers the best hope for success. Try to pick a line that is smooth and has the best traction; it's safer, faster, and requires less energy. To make sure you select the best line, it is better to stop or slow down at the bottom of a hill and take a few seconds to pick a route before you attempt the climb than it is to fail and have to go back down to the bottom and try it again. Of course, once your technical skills improve, many more line options will open up for you.

3. Technique execution
To execute means to apply the correct techniques at the right place and time so that you can stay on the best line you can see. Understanding what to do is one thing, but doing it is another. That's why most sports take practice. You don't swing a tennis racket or golf club correctly until you practice and finally execute what you're trying to do. To execute means to accomplish a desired outcome by following a step-by-step process. You can't ride over that log or climb up that ledge if you don't know how and haven't tried it before. That's what practice is, executing techniques. So to help you execute, we've written this book with step-by-step explanations of how to practice all the important techniques you'll need to ride a dirt bike.

How to practice staying on line
Once you've picked the best line, you must stick to it by applying the right techniques for inch-perfect tire placement to stay on the best line (see Chapter 5). If you can ride on a narrow line you can ride on single-track trails (they look like a cow trail), one of the coolest things you can do on an off-road bike. To practice staying on line we use two 10-foot, 2-by-6-inch boards placed end to end and ask our students to ride all the way down it without coming off the boards. This skill will also help you when trapped in a rut and must stay in the bottom center of it to avoid your tires scrubbing the sides.

We find that many times a crash can be attributed to not picking a good line or not being able to stick to it. We know this because we simply walk up the trail and trace a rider's wheel tracks back from where they crashed. We can see where they ran wide and missed the correct line by an inch. As they continued, this became a foot or two off line, putting them in bad terrain where they eventually crashed. The problem really started up the trail when they missed the right line.

Don't just go riding, go practicing too
"Practice makes perfect" is a tired old adage, but it certainly rings true with the difficult sport of dirt-bike riding. Practice as perfectly as possible—it takes hard practice to make you realize what your riding strengths and weaknesses are. How badly do you want to get better? If you have the desire and good practice ethics, you can improve your skills quickly. Practice ethics are how you approach every ride. To start, don't just go riding, go practicing. Take this book with you the next time you go riding and practice as many exercises as you can, making changes to increase or decrease the challenges to suit your skill level. How often should you practice? Of course, the answer is to practice as much as you can. Unfortunately many busy people only have time to ride two or three times a month. Once you've learned and developed your skills, you have to use them frequently, or as they say, "use it, or lose it."

Most people never practice. They just go riding with the goal of reaching a destination or keeping up with someone. When riding with others, don't try to keep up if they're better than you; they'll respect and appreciate you more if you ride within your limits and avoid injury than if you try to keep up. Concentrate on building your skills and your control; confidence and speed will come soon enough.

Practice like a kid

Kids think they're just playing, but they're actually practicing while having fun pushing their limits. They are good at jumping their bicycles because they practice something they love to do over and over, all while challenging and trying to outperform their buddies. In the dirt bike world, what many call play riding is actually practicing. If adults knew what to practice and had fun practicing like kids do, they could improve as quickly as the kids do. So if you really love riding motorcycles and really want to improve, make practicing fun and you'll never *have to* practice again.

Good practice ethics mean that you must try to define why you ride, how you want to ride, be aware of your skills and abilities (and that of your bike), and stay within them. It doesn't matter what your age is, the same approach applies: You just have to be more patient and deliberate if you start late. Remember, put your brain in gear first, take it step-by-step, experiment, exaggerate, and be sensitive to feel the feedback you get from your bike through your body. If you can, practice a specific technique for at least two consecutive days to really "burn" it into your memory.

Of course, it always helps to ride with people who have more skills than you, and if you race, practice harder than you race and the races will seem easy. It would also be nice if you had a good coach who can spot both good habits and bad habits. Play race with friends. Competition is a great way to improve your skills, gain confidence, and gauge yourself against others in your class.

Use speed as a tool

It's a thrill to go fast, and we all want to know how fast our bikes will go. Speed is good at the right place and time, but it should be only one of many techniques you know. In racing sports like motocross, speed is the name of the game. Most people have developed good techniques and a feel for speed well before they start racing. We recommend that developing riders concentrate on mastering slow and moderate speed techniques first and think of speed as icing on the cake or a bonus. No doubt there are many times, like in hillclimbing, when speed is critical to making it or not, but speed should be a tool you can use when needed, not a crutch you can lean on all the time.

For correct body positioning you must move your body rearward as you ride faster—just don't forget to move back forward when riding slow again. Many times after riding fast people fail to move forward for a slow turn and with no weight on the front tire lose traction and crash to the low side. Off-road riders should constantly move forward and rearward as their speed increases and decreases. When riding at slow to moderate speeds, it's important to ride bowlegged and freely move side to side on the bike. When riding at fast speeds you will move your body slightly less from side to side and will occasionally need to squeeze your legs against the bike to help stabilize it and maintain control.

Speed is actually a stabilizer for a two-wheeled machine. In many cases it's harder to go slow than it is to go fast. However, speed can also be a compensator for someone with inadequate skills or techniques, which of course will eventually spell trouble. The fact is, your spinning wheels create a gyroscopic effect that helps keep you upright.

In easy sections, if you ride fast for a length of time as with many street riders, you can become "velocitized," which causes you to underestimate how long it will take to slow down, which may end up with you overshooting the next corner. Be aware of this phenomenon, and remember the faster you go the more room you'll need to slow down. Generally speaking, most people self-limit their speed and only go as fast as they feel comfortable regardless of their bikes' engine size or capability for speed.

Tales from the Trail:
HOW A LEGEND WAS BORN

During a big off-road race many years ago one of the front runners got stuck on a hill and created a bottleneck with many riders getting stuck behind him. Along comes Malcolm Smith. Because of his great riding skills, he quickly found a way around the bottleneck by riding up a difficult line nobody else would dare try. A collective "who was that guy?" emerged from the crowd, and the word soon spread in the pits. It was his ability to see alternate lines and his outstanding skills that helped Malcolm get through jams like this and how he became one of the true legends of American off-road motorcycle racers.

We believe in learning to walk (ride slowly) before you run (ride fast). Most of the techniques you need to know can be learned and developed at a relatively low speed where mistakes aren't so costly. It's when you ride fast and make a mistake that you really pay for it. Going too fast for a rider's skills or the terrain conditions is possibly the most common cause of motorcycle crashes.

The ultimate perspective

Of course, if you ride motorcycles in the dirt, we must address the real possibility of falling off or crashing.

Old-timers say there are two kinds of motorcycle riders, those who have been down and those who are going down. The reality is, if you're learning, challenging, practicing, and pushing the limit, you will crash occasionally. Dirt is certainly a friendlier and softer place to learn to ride than the street and that is another reason why experts agree that dirt is the best place to learn to ride a motorcycle.

Crashing is an important part of the learning process if you want to become a good rider. If you want to improve you will have to push the limits to gain a true perspective

Play Racing

1 For a fun *and* skill building exercise try racing around a tight flat oval course with a friend like we are doing here on equal Yamaha TTR125s.

2 All you need is an apex marker or two.

Tales from the Trail:
FASTER ISN'T ALWAYS BETTER

This story was told by Dave Pyle, Larry Roeseler's Kawasaki Team Green mechanic back when Roeseler was winning Baja 1000 races and many others races too. One day Pyle brought Roeseler out to ride trials with us and everybody was amazed at how good he was. Pyle was a good trials rider himself and wasn't surprised to hear this. He said that Roeseler had always ridden like a trials rider, but up to this point had only a KX500 to ride. Pyle went on to explain that Roeseler on his KX500 was as fast as anyone in the fast parts of the race, probably even faster, but he knew when to slow down and how to ride through tough technical terrain. He said it's as if he had a rheostat knob on his brain that he would reach up and change from full-tilt racer to technical trials rider and then back again as needed. Great riders like Roeseler know when they can go fast *and* when they need to slow down and avoid mistakes.

of what is too much and what is not enough. When you're learning you shouldn't be worried or afraid to make a mistake and possibly crash or damage your motorcycle (at lower speeds, we hope). Off-road bikes are designed for crashing and usually come out unscathed when crashed (well, you'll probably get some cosmetic damage pretty quickly). Crashing a street or dual-sport bike is much more costly. Scratched, bent, and broken parts are small consequences of the learning process. Motorcycle racers know this and are always pushing the limits and expect to occasionally crash. Professional riders know if they don't crash occasionally they're not pushing their limits and may not be improving their skills.

If you know you're going to crash be sure to shut the throttle off; gassing it at that point will only make the crash worse. If you crash, try to absorb the landing like a gymnast would by tucking and rolling as opposed to trying to stop your body by "pancaking" with outstretched arms and legs. After first making sure you're okay, pick up the bike and check it out to make sure it's okay before you start it up and take off again. When picking up your bike, squat down, stand up, and use your legs, not your back. The technique for

3 Keep your cool if you happen to get a little close to each other.

4 As you exit the corner, get your weight back and gradually turn on the power.

Tales from the Trail:
THE MATHEMATICAL APPROACH TO RIDING

Over the years, there have been many good books written about how to ride a motorcycle, but one in particular really takes the cake. It was written by engineers to mathematically explain how the rider and motorcycle "system" works together to do what it does. I know this from when I worked at American Honda in its Product Evaluation Department and one day found an SAE technical report on my desk with a note on it from my boss that jokingly said, "This is what I think about when I ride." The report was written in 1984 by Honda engineers and was titled "Equations of Longitudinal Motion for the Rider/Motorcycle System." It is filled with calculations I couldn't begin to understand. Look it up; it is an amazing study written by and for someone far smarter than me.

This is the correct sit-down riding position for a tight turn with the rider sitting forward, leg and foot out and forward, leaning the bike and turning the handlebars, with the rider's shoulders staying parallel with the handlebars.

This rider is confused and thinks he is road racing by leaning his body into the turn and not the bike. He should save this technique for riding his sport bike on track days.

Counterbalancing is king when riding in technical terrain at slower speeds. Keep your weight over your feet, lean your bike one way and shift your hips the other way, stay centered, and keep your shoulders square to the handlebars. This simple skill is a gateway key to helping many riders overcome a major plateau in their riding skills.

picking up big dual-sport bikes is to turn around and lean into the bike as you squat and stand.

Next, check the twist throttle on the handlebar. Does it open *and* close freely, or is it stuffed with sand and mud and need to be cleaned before using? (Check the throttle cable[s] too.) How are the handlebars and front forks aligned? On many small bikes they can twist in a crash and become misaligned, but can usually be easily straightened by twisting the handlebars while bumping the front wheel into an immovable object. If your bars are bent they need to be replaced when you get home. Check the clutch, brake and shift levers, and rear brake pedal. If you lay your bike down, gas might spill out of your carburetor overflow tube. So if you crash, be sure to quickly pick your bike up and keep that valuable gas where it should be. You'll need it to get home. If you have to lay your bike down on purpose, simply turn off the gas petcock to prevent the carburetor from overflowing and spilling gas (just don't forget to turn it back on).

If you do happen to crash, before you take off again, first try to understand why you crashed. Was it because you misjudged? Was it because you didn't see something you should have? Did you stray off your line? If you can pinpoint the reason for crashing you can avoid making the same mistake again.

Continue developing your skills

If you want to take your riding to the next level, but are having trouble, you may have reached a "skills plateau" because you lack certain "gateway" or key skills. You may be fundamentally flawed and you'll know it, especially if you compete and get beat a lot. This is when training and a good coach can make a big difference and really help you speed up the learning process.

Off-road motorcycle competition

I always say one of the best ways to test and improve your riding skills is to compete. There are many forms of off-road motorcycle competition today and many annual events that you can enter to compete for the title of local, state, regional, or even national champion. There are both Amateur and Professional classes and often competition classes for youth, women, and veterans where you race people your own age. Typically classes are set by engine size and rider skill levels, such as novice, sportsman, intermediate, advanced, expert, master, and professional. There is an off-road motorcycle-racing series and class for almost everyone,

This is a good hand grip to help you hang onto your bike's handlebars and still operate the clutch, front brake, and throttle. With two fingers operating the levers your other two fingers and thumb can wrap around and maintain a good grip for the rugged off-road conditions.

Flattrack racing is just one of the many forms of motorcycle competitions found throughout the country. Many beginning racers start with enduros or cross country or motocross.

and we highly recommend that you get involved in racing after developing the basic skills outlined in this book. As an added bonus, you'll meet the nicest people and make new friends at the motorcycle races.

In this book we do not attempt to cover all the techniques and knowledge it requires to race all these different motorcycle sports. We cover the basics for motocross and trials, but will save dwelling into the complicated world

of expert-level racing techniques and requirements for another book.

The wide range of off-road motorcycle racing offered in America is incredible. There's motocross and supercross, desert racing, enduros, cross country, endurocross, hillclimbs, observed trials, flat track, speedway, SuperMoto, and even ice racing. In addition, there are also many forms of vintage bike racing, which has become quite popular in the last few decades.

Tales from the Trail:
FOR MAXIMUM SATISFACTION, RACE A BIKE YOU CAN HANDLE

Years ago I was invited to race a vintage motocross aboard a Bultaco 360 Pursang in the Open Expert Class. I couldn't pass it up. The day was fun and the racing was fast and furious with the track groomed to accommodate the limited suspension of the old vintage bikes. This experience reminded me about how much bikes have evolved and the incredible capabilities of modern open class (450cc) bikes. So much so that the average racer can't come close to riding one to its limits. Modern bikes are built to take the punishment of a pro and they laugh at the average rider. Riding these high-performance modern machines well requires tremendous physical conditioning. At this vintage race I was able to ride that old Bultaco hard all day and wring every ounce of performance out of it. It was very satisfying as opposed to riding a modern bike that for most is downright intimidating. If you're thinking about purchasing that 450cc four-stroke motocross bike, you might reconsider and go for a 250cc four-stroke instead. It will likely be a more satisfying experience.

4 Body Positioning

Correct body positioning is critical to riding off-road well

Correct body positioning and weight shifting when riding is essential to succeed in any exercise or challenging riding situation. We find that many new riders often have a tendency to tense up their upper bodies and slide back or migrate rearward, especially in challenging riding situations. At MotoVentures we spend considerable time reminding our students that there are a lot of riding situations where it's important to have your body forward. In this chapter we will point out the value and benefits of correct body positioning.

As unusual as it seems, lots of off-road riding situations require that you ride standing up. When riding standing up, you will be in one of two basic riding positions: the attack position and the energy-conserving position. Riding standing up actually improves a bike's handling by lowering the center of mass.

The correct weight shifting will dramatically improve your bike's handling. There are actually three directions of movement you can make with your body while riding: up and down, forward and back, and side to side. Try to keep your legs active and even overexaggerate at times. Ride slightly bowlegged and counterbalance when needed. Generally speaking, you should gradually shift your body rearward as you ride faster and forward as you ride slower. It's all about whether you want weight over the front end for turning traction or weight over the rear end for power-to-the-ground traction.

"While fitness is crucial to riding at the top level, equally important is economy of motion. Learning how to properly use balance and leverage to minimize your muscle energy output will enable you to go just as fast at the end of a ride or race as in the beginning. Being less fatigued also minimizes your chances of making a mistake."

Lee Parks
Best-selling author of Total Control, founder of Total Control Training, 2001 WERA National Endurance champion, second-place finisher in 1994 AMA 125GP national championship

Correct body positioning can be perfected by practicing every time you ride until it becomes automatic and natural. Learning correct body positioning will create that all-important muscle memory and feeling sensations that you will recognize every time you ride. Remember, always think of how you can position your body to help get your bike over, around, or through a difficult situation.

Sitting position

Everyone starts riding motorcycles by riding in the sitting position. Standing comes after you're comfortable with the controls. Of course, there is a right way to sit and a wrong way. For example, many people make the mistake when riding off-road of sitting in one place all the time. It's important to move back and forth on the seat to shift your weight and help traction on the front or rear tires.

Sitting is totally appropriate for certain situations like braking, turns, and starts. If you are climbing while sitting down, don't slide back on the seat. It will cause your bike

This is the attack position as demonstrated statically with the bike on a stand. In this position the rider is fully coiled and poised to spring and attack challenging terrain, especially when riding at speed.

to do a wheelie and you will lose control. When climbing a hill, you may start out by standing but may eventually end up sitting near the top. Riding sitting down connects all your body weight to the bike. The problem with this position is when you hit a bump the jolt is transferred through your torso to your upper body and arms and can cause the dreaded "butt steer," which is when the bike steers you instead of you steering the bike.

You ride sitting down where you can to conserve energy, as in racing when constant acceleration is pulling hard on your arms. Sitting is what you do where appropriate and when you are riding casually or when you just can't, or don't want to, stand up anymore.

Standing position

If you plan to do any serious off-road riding you should learn how to ride standing up. There are basically two positions to choose from while riding standing up: the attack position and the energy conservation mode (see the following descriptions). When you ride off-road standing up you should stay a little bowlegged and only connect to the bike in four places, with your two hands and two feet, so you can avoid butt steer (see Chapter 8). In the more extreme world of off-road or motocross racing it is sometimes helpful to temporarily grip the tank with your knees to help maintain control.

Riding while standing up places all of your body weight on the footpegs instead of the seat and actually lowers your overall center of mass. Riding standing up allows riders to steer the bike with their legs and feet by shifting weight to create more or less bike lean angle. The better the rider the more active their legs, which allows them to spring, absorb, counterbalance, and quickly adjust their riding position in any direction to better deal with the rapidly changing terrain. Learn how to ride standing up correctly so you can be more proactive to terrain, not reactive, and you'll be able to ride better and longer. Note: Riding standing up will cause your left boot sole to wear out in the arch because you will constantly grind it on the left footpeg when shifting. You can always tell if someone spends a lot of time standing up by just looking at their boot soles.

How to shift gears while standing up

To shift gears while standing you may have to shift your weight to your right leg momentarily in order to move your left ankle or lift your left leg to shift the gear lever as needed. When you first start riding standing up you may need to think about it, but it eventually becomes second nature.

This is the attack riding position in action. With your legs and arms fully coiled like this you are ready to attack any rough terrain challenge that you may come across.

The attack position

The name says it all: The attack position is used to "attack" just about any tough terrain up ahead (bumps, rocks, water, mud, and so on) or at the beginning of just about any technical maneuver you are about to attempt (jumps, hillclimbs, super tight single tracks, and so on). The attack position is when you're standing up, fully poised and coiled, with knees, waist, and arms bent and ready to either quickly spring or absorb in reaction to fast-approaching challenges. To get a good feel for what the attack position looks like, watch any motocrosser as he or she approaches a whoop section and most of the time they'll be in the attack position. The problem is most people can't ride for long in the attack position as it will quickly wear them out. Part of the trick to making it through a long day of riding is knowing when to ride in the attack position and when to ride in the energy conservation mode.

The energy conservation position

Many people don't know or understand the energy conservation position and that is the reason why they poop out early when they ride (bet you never knew how physically demanding off-road riding actually is). Veteran riders certainly know this trick and use it to keep riding fast for long periods. They go into, and out of, the attack position as needed, and then they ride in the energy conservation position the rest of the time.

To practice riding in the energy conservation position, stand up and try to carry your weight primarily with your feet and legs. That way your upper body is freed up to deal only with managing the handlebar controls. If you try to hold yourself up with your arms, you may have throttle control problems and you will wear yourself out prematurely.

As you accelerate in the energy conservation position you need to bend at the waist and arms and lean your torso a little forward into the wind against your chest and with the force of your acceleration going against your legs and footpegs and not your arms. At times you may lean so much forward that you will have your chest over the handlebars. In the energy conservation position you can straighten out your back (unlike the attack position), but be sure to keep your knees slightly bent and bowlegged. Really good riders are proactive and actually lean forward slightly before applying the throttle to ensure the acceleration forces are carried by their legs and not their arms.

This is the energy conserving riding position. Many people haven't discovered this position yet and suffer by prematurely getting tired. In this position you will stand more upright, but lean forward, into the wind as you accelerate, keeping your weight over the foot pegs and not on your arms.

This is the energy conserving position in action. In this position the rider actually leans forward slightly over the front of the bike. In this position when they accelerate they are braced for it so it won't strain their arms.

Weight shifting

There's no such thing as moving too much on a dirt bike. A rider's body weight is a big percentage of the overall weight of the bike and rider. Therefore, when a rider shifts his or her weight at the right time and place, it can have a dramatic effect on the handling of the bike. Watch good riders closely. They're constantly moving around to help their bikes get through a section as smoothly as possible (they aren't just showing off by moving around so much). You'll be a more successful rider if you always think in terms of how moving your body around can help the bike get through, over, and around a challenging situation. Work with your bike's suspension movements, not against them. A lot of learning how to do this is simply getting a lot of seat time out on the trail. If you can learn to coordinate your weight shifting with the movements of the suspension, and add good timing, control coordination, and judgment, you will soon be able to rip like a pro.

Move your body in three directions

There are basically three directions, or axis, that riders can move or shift their bodies on a motorcycle. The first is up and down (or standing and sitting), which is essential for rough off-road riding situations. The second direction is moving forward and rearward, which is used for turning, climbing, and soft terrain. The third direction is moving from side to side, which comes in handy for staying on line or riding single track, through rain ruts or sand washes, at a slow speed while turning and standing up, while hillclimbing,

and on sidehills. This side-to-side direction, more than the other two, is all too often misunderstood or not used and really holds people back. Perfect this skill and people will start calling you a technical rider. At MotoVentures we found that when we teach this skill and the students demonstrate it, they sometimes forget to do it when out on a trail ride and "center up" again. Concentrating on riding a little bowlegged helps you to get in the mode of using side-to-side weight transfer.

Ride a little bowlegged

When you ride standing up, especially in technical terrain, we recommend that you ride with your legs a little bowlegged so you won't inhibit the bike's lean angle, or transfer the bike's movement to yourself. Riding slightly bowlegged will allow the bike to float between your legs. Gripping the bike with your knees is useful in certain situations like motocross whoops, ruts, or jumps, but generally when riding standing up try to only connect to the bike in four places (your hands and feet), not six. This allows the rider to disconnect from the bike and create an isolation or buffer between themselves and the bike so they can control it as opposed to having it bump against and control them. To practice riding bowlegged, see how to counterbalance turns in Chapter 5.

Ride with active legs and feet

Active legs are one of the keys to achieving greater results from your dirt-bike riding. When standing you can use your legs to spring, absorb, shift, counterbalance, transfer weight to either wheel quickly, change lines, and so on. Our legs have the biggest muscles in our body and for

Leaning forward while standing allows you to place your weight over the front tire for better grip and allows you to carry your body weight with your legs when accelerating (not with your arms).

many riders are mostly underutilized when they ride. Done correctly, you can actually steer your bike with your lower body, and not your arms. Use footpeg pressure to help lean the bike for turning while standing. Avoid putting too much pressure on your upper body—keep it relaxed so you can operate the throttle, front brake, and clutch correctly. Your upper body is only capable of handling stress and strain for a short time. The more you use your legs, the better rider you will be.

Ride with your feet up

Except for certain racing techniques used in flat-track, moto-cross, and free-style motocross, it is usually better to ride a motorcycle with your feet on the footpegs and not flailing about. Every time you put your foot out you use more energy and expose your feet and legs to injuries. Keeping your feet up will help you maintain control of the bike and will make the bike handle better too because all your weight will be placed at the lowest point on the bike for a reduced center of mass. If you must put your foot down, and you're not going too fast, try to use it to regain your balance and push off or reposition your body. Don't just tap it down, dangle it, or drag it behind you.

Over-exaggerate your movements

When learning new techniques, we recommend that you over-exaggerate your body movements so that you can gain the important perspective of what is too much and what is not

enough so you can feel what we call the "sweet spot." Your body will tell you: move too far and you'll feel awkward; back off 10 percent and we bet you'll have it just right.

Additional tips on body positions and bike controls

*   ***Clutch:*** A dirt bike's clutch can be used for much more than stopping, starting, and shifting gears. Consider your clutch "an additional control device" that can also be used to gain or prevent traction, slow down, pause, or speed up, and most effectively, apply a sudden burst of power. On most bikes it doesn't take much of a pull on the clutch lever to quickly gain engine rpm so you can make a jump or keep your engine from stalling while braking or descending. You can use your entire hand on the lever when stopping or starting; otherwise you can simply reach out and handle the clutch with just two fingers (the index and middle fingers). The reason most expert riders do this is so they can be ready to pull it in if needed, while still maintaining a good grip on the handlebars with the thumb and the other two fingers.

Note: You should position your front brake and clutch levers, shift lever, and brake pedal so they are comfortable in both the sitting and standing riding positions for you. You can also rotate the handlebars slightly forward for more comfort when standing or slightly rearward to be more comfortable when sitting.

Note: Once you conquer basic shifting skills and become more confident, you can try shifting with a minimum

Sitting rearward is relaxing when you're on "cruise mode." Just remember, in this position you have plenty of weight on the rear tire, but very little weight over the front tire so you could lose traction on it more easily in a turn or loop over rearward more easily on a hillclimb.

Sit forward for tight flat turns, up hills, when releasing the clutch to take off, and when coming to a stop. In this position your front tire has enough weight on it to grip the ground in turns.

clutch pull or without using the clutch at all by shutting off the throttle and quickly "snicking" it into the next gear. The gearbox on most bikes can handle clutchless shifting, but be careful since doing it incorrectly can damage your transmission (you'll usually hear some ugly noises if you are doing it wrong).

• **Throttle:** If you find your throttle hand is tiring or you're having trouble controlling your throttle, you may be placing too much pressure on your right arm, often from sitting or leaning too rearward. If you accelerate suddenly, and you're not quite ready for it, the acceleration can pull your body rearward and the force is too great for you to shut the throttle off. This is colorfully called "whiskey throttle" or "wrist lock" and the way to avoid it is to sit more forward and lean forward and keep a bend in your arms. When first learning it is a good idea to make sure you don't overgrip the throttle or raise your wrist up so you can twist the grip more or faster. It is better to keep your wrist in line with your arm to help you control the throttle.

Practice counterbalancing turns by starting with wide 180-degree turns in each direction.

This photo shows a rider practicing how to stay on a relatively straight line like the bottom of a rain rut or on a narrow single tack trail at a relatively slow speed. He is steering his bike by leaning it rather than turning his handlebars and every time he leans the bike to steer it he must extend his knee and shift his hip over and counterbalance to keep from falling over.

Another common throttle problem for new riders is when they inadvertently turn on the throttle when applying the front brake. The trouble is, they aren't separating the two different motions of the wrist and fingers. The cure for this is to simply remember to raise your right elbow a little when shutting off the throttle just before applying the front brake. This will help separate those two different movements.

• **Front and rear brakes:** When using the front brake it is important to simultaneously maintain a grip with that hand so if you hit a bump the handlebars won't be jolted out of your hands. This can be accomplished by using two fingers only (preferably your index and middle fingers) for the front brake when riding so your thumb and other two fingers are constantly gripping the handlebars, just like with the throttle. Two fingers will provide plenty of power for today's bikes, and when riding slowly, even one finger will do.

Position your rear brake pedal height where you like it, usually a little high for those who ride standing a lot, a little low for those who ride sitting a lot, or better yet, in a position that can be used both sitting and standing. Learn how to cover the rear brake and try to develop a feel for when the wheel will lock up, which is tough to get used to with today's stiff protective boots. Be sure not to stand on the brake pedal or drag the brake. When not using the rear brake, slide your foot to the side slightly, but don't stick your feet out too far and risk catching them on a rock or bush as you ride by. As your riding confidence and skills improve you can actually become so proficient at using all the controls you will be able to use some of them simultaneously (eventually, you'll have to).

- **Legs and knees:** It's okay to momentarily squeeze or grip the gas tank with your legs, especially in racing situations like motocross, but usually in technical riding it is best to keep your legs slightly bent and bowlegged and limit your contact to the bike to primarily your hands and feet so you can isolate your body movements from the bike's movements. Strong and active legs are the key to being a really good off-road rider who will use them to squat and soak up or absorb a bump or spring to take weight off the rear or load the suspension to get more height or distance when jumping. The faster you ride, the more you can start using your legs and knees to squeeze or lean against the bike to control it like you must do to ride motocross.

- **Arms and elbows:** When riding off-road it's okay to straighten your arms momentarily, but usually it is best to keep them bent. This ensures a forward lean and will help you maintain good throttle control. Holding your elbows up is good if you have the energy, but can be tiring and unnecessary in many cases where you could be saving energy.

- **Feet:** You can move your foot placement on the footpegs from your arches to the balls of your feet, but primarily use your arches when jumping. When shifting, move your foot to the side out of the way after shifting, and don't look down to shift or brake. To shift gears while riding standing up you will need to shift your weight momentarily to your right leg so you can lift your leg and move your foot as needed to shift the next gear, then resume standing on both pegs. Practice this and it will become seamless.

When using the rear brake you can cover the pedal with your right foot so you're ready to use it, as long as you don't drag it too much or try to stand on it. Covering

You can really help someone experience counterbalancing without riding by holding them like this and having them correctly position their body. Once set, ask them to mentally "take a picture" of that position so they can return to it when riding.

Try 360-degree turns, full lock if you can.

the rear brake is the secret to prevent you from going over backward when performing a wheelie while sitting down. Be cautious about sticking your feet out sideways too much from your footpegs. That makes them vulnerable to hitting rocks and other hazards and could result in a broken toe or twisted ankle.

- **Shoulders:** Always keep your shoulders parallel to the handlebar crossbar (as it turns) when going around a corner. Squaring up like this helps correctly position your entire body to the direction change. Squaring up your shoulders will help keep you from drifting wide in corners, especially on the corner exits.

- **Hips:** Of course you can shift your hips forward or rearward to corner, climb, or descend, but don't forget you can also shift your hips sideways in the opposite direction of the bike's lean to counterbalance, steer, or stay on line. Don't fool yourself, twisting your body doesn't help. You must shift your hips sideways. Your ability to shift your body sideways is one of the keys to riding off-road well.

5 Braking

You won't ride fast until you're confident you can slow down

Slowing and stopping quickly and effectively is just as important while trail riding as getting power to the ground. In this chapter, we'll learn the correct techniques of off-road motorcycle braking. Unlike a car where one brake pedal controls the brakes on all four wheels, motorcycle riders must operate the two brakes on their machines separately. It's not because the manufacturers can't make a one-lever braking system, but rather because having control of the brakes separately allows the rider to choose exactly when, and how much, each brake is applied, which is critical to effective and safe off-roading.

Contrary to what one might think, the front brake is the more effective of the two, providing approximately 80 percent of the stopping power. The problem is new riders don't have an instinctive feel for using the front brake, and with everything they're trying to learn and process on those first rides, it's easy for them to forget to use the front brake. In an emergency situation you only have a split second to react correctly so it is critical that you learn the correct braking techniques or you could inadvertently crash while trying to avoid a crash.

The front brake is quite tricky to use at first, so it's best for beginners to use the rear brake on their first rides, until they have plenty of control stopping on flat, easy surfaces at moderate speeds. But it's still important to learn how to use the front brake as soon as possible. Master the front brake and you'll be able to ride safer, faster, and you will no longer fear downhills.

"Improving your braking technique is directly tied to having the correct body position. Go out and practice on a wide variety of terrain and learn where to position your body when braking in sand, down hills, hard pack, off-cambers, and more. Those important skills are the keys to building riding confidence and are the building blocks for off-road speed."

Andy Jefferson
AMA National Motocross/Supercross racer

The goal of this braking exercise is to develop your braking feel, skills, and judgment to confidently operate at the threshold of lock-up with the front wheel, which is the point of maximum braking efficiency. Once the front wheel locks up, you have crossed that threshold and will start losing braking efficiency and steering control as well. The only way to safely learn the limits of braking is to gradually approach the limit, gently exceed the limit, then back off a little so you can operate consistently close to the limit.

Note: Be sure to adjust your front brake lever and rear brake pedal so you can reach them comfortably when riding standing up, sitting down, leaning forward for uphills, or leaning rearward for downhills. Make sure the front brake lever is adjusted correctly so it can be used with two fingers and will not press down on your other two fingers when applied.

How to practice braking

To practice braking, you must first locate a flat, smooth, hard-packed dirt straightaway. Pick a clear point or place where you want to stop and mark it with some easy-to-see object. This first exercise is done while sitting down. Start from about 80 yards back, pick up plenty of speed, shifting to at least third so that you will have to squeeze the brakes progressively for a good distance. Once up to speed, pull

in the clutch (use your whole hand and don't downshift) and apply the rear brake only. Using the rear brake only, you'll find it is easy to lock up the rear tire and very easy to get sideways if you slide it and lean a little. This is why it is important that you keep the bike perpendicular to the ground and with the wheels in line as much as possible. When you become sideways you'll be forced to lay off both brakes, especially the front brake, which of course is counterproductive and the opposite of what you're trying to do.

Next, start using both brakes at the same time, eventually with emphasis on using the front brake firmly. Each time you make a pass, once you begin braking come to a complete stop. If you stop short of your mark, you need to adjust your judgment on the next pass so you will stop where you want to stop. Once people start using the front brake correctly, they are surprised at how quickly their bike will stop. Just make sure you achieve the *first goal* of stopping as quickly as possible, then achieve the *second goal* of combining that newfound braking feel with your good judgment on distance and you'll discover you can stop almost anywhere, anytime you want to stop, literally on a dime.

Operate the front brake by using only two fingers. We recommend the index and middle finger, which leaves your third finger, little finger, and thumb to hold onto the handlebars. This way, if you hit a bump when using the

Sloppy Braking

1 Sloppy braking like this lengthens the distance it takes to stop.

2 This rider has leaned the bike slightly and the rear wheel has stepped sideways, forcing him to back off the front brake, which is counterproductive.

On a firm, smooth dirt surface pick up good speed (third gear), pull in the clutch, wait a split-second, apply both brakes progressively, and be sure to keep the bike perpendicular to the ground, the handlebars straight, and the wheels in line.

Proper Braking

1 Truly efficient braking requires that you keep your wheels in line, keep the bike perpendicular to the ground, ...

2 ... keep the handlebars straight, and develop a tremendous feel for the threshold of lock-up.

front brake, you won't lose your grip on the handlebars. Most of today's bikes have plenty of braking power that only requires two fingers. Any more would overpower the front brake and be harder to modulate under hard braking. You can maintain a normal grip on the throttle when riding around, but to use the front brake reach out with only two fingers. You'll see racers ride with two fingers on the front brake constantly and you'll see them use only one finger when riding slow technical terrain. This split-finger grip is also good for street-bike and dual-sport riders who must operate on increasingly pot-holed, rock-strewn roads. There is no more helpless feeling than hitting a hole or rock you didn't see and having your handlebars ripped violently out of your hands while riding. Trust me.

With each pass, go a little faster, brake a little later, and at your own comfort level, gradually squeeze the front brake lever harder each time. You don't have to pull the clutch in and hit the brakes simultaneously. Pull in the clutch and wait a microsecond, then apply the brakes. Once you start braking, continue to progressively squeeze harder until you come to a complete stop. Your front forks should remain compressed throughout the process and you should take a slightly different line on each pass so the grooves made by previous passes won't affect your braking.

Note: If you find yourself twisting the throttle when using the front brake, try raising your right elbow just as you begin using the front brake. Doing so helps separate the two motions of twisting and squeezing that your right hand must accomplish.

When you brake hard you'll know it when the front brake rotor starts moaning or squealing and by the sight of your front wheel actually slowing and even locking-up momentarily just before you stop. Remember, lock-up should only occur at the tail end of braking. You can't go far with the front tire locked up before losing control. When you are pushing the limits and the front wheel does lock up, try to keep your handlebars relatively straight and you will usually have two choices. Instinctively, most people will release the brake, which immediately straightens out the bike and you might travel beyond your braking point. The only other thing that you can do to maintain control when the front wheel locks up is to lean your body off slightly to one side or the other side of the bike (very advanced) to keep the bike absolutely perpendicular to the ground. You know you're a braking demon when you can confidently and consistently brake at or near the threshold of lock-up in a variety of terrain without crashing.

What about the rear brake?

When you really want to stop quickly in a straight line, the correct way is to hammer on both brakes. When you would like the back end to slide around a corner, use just the rear brake to break the rear tire loose as you begin your turn (see Chapter 16, which details brake sliding). The rear brake also comes in handy when riding in soft terrain like sand where the front tire will dig in and grab too much if the front brake is applied. The rear brake should also be favored when going down hills where the terrain is too steep and loose for hard front wheel braking.

Body positioning for braking

The reason the front brake has most of the stopping power isn't because the brake itself is better but because most of the bike and rider's weight goes to the front end when stopping. To counter that when braking aggressively, riders should always keep their arms and legs slightly bent, but shift their weight slightly rearward to counter the braking forces, give the rear tire some traction, and keep the rear end on the ground.

Tales from the Trail:
SLOW DOWN TO GO FAST

Many riders don't use their brakes to their fullest potential. Once we show them the correct way at MotoVentures, people are surprised at how quickly they can stop once they know the proper techniques. When they go out to ride again at their favorite track or trails, we often get an email from them basically saying that since we taught them how to slow down and stop quickly, they now feel more comfortable and are actually riding much faster. Isn't it interesting how their lack of braking skills was holding them back from riding fast?

Advanced stopping practice:

- Try hard braking while riding standing up and see how you must shift rearward to counter the braking forces.
- Try braking while going down a steep, loose hill and see how slowly you can crawl to the bottom.
- On a flat, hardpacked area, try braking with the rear brake only, then front brake only, to feel the difference.

- Try braking by pitching the bike sideways, then again by keeping the wheels in line, and see which way stops you quicker.
- Practice braking in sand, mud, and other soft conditions. See how you can rely more on the rear brake in these situations.
- Try threshold front braking on a high-traction surface, but be careful and progressive with your braking.

Nose Wheelies

1 Nose wheelies are easy to perform when riding downhill on a full traction concrete slab like this one.

2 They are a fun way to help develop your feel for threshold braking and...

3 ...also experimenting with balance points too.

4 Back and safe on the concrete.

6 Turning

Perfect these turning fundamentals and you will lead instead of follow

Turning is where many people struggle in the dirt, and like everything else, it's all about having sound fundamentals to perform it correctly. In this chapter we will learn the basics of turning, first while riding sitting down, then while riding standing up. Each requires two simple, but distinctly different, techniques. First, it is important to understand the three basic ways, or combinations of ways, that motorcycles turn:

1. By turning the handlebars (at slow speed)

2. By leaning the motorcycle (at mid to high speed)

3. By sliding the rear tire (at any speed)

We'll teach you how to turn all three ways, but of these three you will probably spend most of your time at mid to high speeds, which requires you to lean your motorcycle to turn it. With leaning skills being so important, make sure to master leaning while standing, sitting, and in all terrain conditions.

"A typical turn can be broken up into three parts: entry, apex, and exit. A common mistake for even the very best riders is to over-rush the entry in an effort to make time, or not putting enough emphasis on an apex in a rush to get back on the throttle and then running wide. These impatient moves will slow what is by far the most important opportunity to make time on the race track, the corner exit. A great drive off the exit will carry you all the way to the checkered flag."

Eric Bostrom

46 AMA National Road Race victories, AMA 600cc National SuperSport Champion, AMA Formula Extreme Champion, AMA SuperTwins Champion, AMA 883 National Dirt Track Champion

Note: Turning a motorcycle places a high demand on your tires, especially the front tire. Make sure to always run the correct air pressures in your tires and, if you can, run fresh tires for the best grip. To ride a motorcycle well requires that you can trust your tires to grip the ground, especially the front tire.

Right turns vs. left turns

We find that many right-handed people have more difficulty with right turns than left turns. Regardless of whether you're right-handed or left-handed, chances are you will have a weak side, or turning direction, and we recommend that you practice and strengthen it rather than ignore it. One theory for this phenomenon is that people tend to lead slightly with their "strong side" and therefore favor one side over the other, resulting in more comfort turning than in their "weak side" direction.

Square your shoulders

Whenever turning while sitting or standing, make sure you square your shoulders to the handlebars. To do this, imagine a straight line across your chest from shoulder to shoulder and keep it parallel to the handlebars as they turn. Do you ever find it hard to make tight turns? Do you ever run wide on flat turns or ride up the raised turns on a motocross track? We call it getting crossed up with your body pointed one way and your bike pointed the other. This technique of shifting your shoulders will also help shift your lower body into a more correct counterbalancing position when riding standing up.

Sit-down turns

New riders spend much of their time sitting instead of standing until they learn how to ride standing up. As mentioned previously there is nothing wrong with riding a bike sitting down, as long as you keep in mind that your performance capabilities are limited when the terrain gets rougher. Sit-down turns are appropriate in many riding and racing situations, however.

Sit-down Turns

1 Approach a tight turn like this sitting down. Be sure to slide forward on the seat, shift down to first or second, and gradually apply the brakes.

2 Lean the bike, extend your leg out in front, square your shoulders, and turn the handlebars.

3 After the apex, accelerate away and slide rearward on the seat. Repeat for the next turn.

Slow, Standing Turns

1 Sometimes on tight trails or on trails with a lot of obstacles, you'll need to perform a slow, standing-up turn.

2 When doing a counterbalance turn, start by leaning your motorcycle and then immediately counterbalance by shifting your hips and body in the opposite direction.

3 Keep your balance, and if there are lots of obstacles, watch where your front tire goes.

4 Begin to finish the turn by straightening up the bike and begin to settle down back in the saddle.

Move your butt

The most common mistake made while turning sitting down is when riders fail to move forward and rearward on the seat and bike. Sliding forward and leaning forward at the right time in a turn will place more weight on the front tire for improved traction. Riders freeze or stop moving forward and rearward and eventually crash when their front tires wash out (slide) in a turn. You must control the front tire first and move rearward on the seat only after you have confidence with the front tire traction.

How to practice sit-down turns

To practice turns while sitting down, locate a flat and firm (high-traction) dirt surface and place an apex marker, like a cone or old tire, to mark your turn. As you approach the turn, shift down to first gear, apply the brakes, and slide your butt forward on the seat. Do all your braking while you are traveling straight, and then let off the brakes to start the turn. Next, put your inside leg out and forward to help lean the bike and to put on the ground if your tires slip or get caught in a rut. Then lean the motorcycle and turn the handlebars. As you do, cover the clutch with one or two fingers in case you need to use it to slow down, stop, or raise the rpm for faster acceleration out of the turn. As you turn, you can also lean forward with your torso at the right moment to help transfer weight to the front tire for added traction. Keep your elbows bent and up.

Don't forget that while turning, either sitting or standing, always keep your shoulders parallel or squared to the handlebars. As you exit the turn, shift up and accelerate, sliding back on the seat to help your bike get traction on the rear wheel. Make sure that you shift down and slide forward again for the next turn. Practice this in both right and left turns.

For a fun advanced turning exercise, try flat tracking around a short dirt oval. Flat tracking combines all the turning skills needed, such as braking and sliding the entrances, leaning and body positions, and powersliding the exit of the turn. To take this exercise to the next level, just pick up the pace and throw in a friend to ride around with and you can practice a little race craft too. See Chapter 17 for how to practice power sliding.

How to practice stand-up turns and counterbalancing

Counterbalancing is simply the art of keeping your balance while riding, especially standing up while turning. In fact, when riding a motorcycle you're always doing some type of counterbalancing. For example, when you ride uphill and lean forward, you are counterbalancing, and when you ride downhill and lean rearward, you are counterbalancing. When you ride a motorcycle off-road you're constantly counterbalancing some terrain challenge. Rarely is it ever flat and smooth; it's usually up, down, or across and rocky, rutted, and bumpy—*and that's why counterbalancing is the king of technical off-road riding skills.*

To practice stand-up turning and counterbalancing, first enlist some help from a strong friend to hold you up while adjusting your body to the correct counterbalancing body position for either a right or left turn. Once positioned correctly, *take a mental picture of yourself* so you can remember and return to that correct position when you ride. Next, locate a flat turn with an apex marker to turn around. Imagine you're in a rutted, rocky, sandy environment and you must ride standing up, but you must negotiate a tight turn at low speed. Approach the turn standing up with your weight centered on the footpegs. Begin by first leaning your bike in the direction you want to turn and immediately countering that lean by shifting your hips in the other direction and moving your outside knee away from the bike, which will also help shift your hips over where they should be.

Remember, to counterbalance correctly you must shift your hips and body in the opposite direction of the way the bike is leaning. Twisting doesn't count for counter balancing. Also, remember to move your body to the side and not too rearward, or you will place too much pressure on your arms. Be sure to square your

Spin Turns

1 If you're at a place where the terrain isn't too sensitive you can make a spin turn by riding in first gear, ...

2 ...sitting forward, extending your leg and placing it on the ground, ...

3 ...lean the bike, turn the handlebars, pull in the clutch to raise the engine rpms and release it to spin the rear wheel, ...

4 ...which quickly rotates the bike 180 degrees.

shoulders to the handlebars just as you must do for sit-down turns. While practicing this, if you keep losing your balance to the inside of the turn and must put your foot down to catch yourself, you're simply not counterbalancing enough.

Note: When practicing high-performance turns, it is better to err on the side of leaning the bike too much than not enough. It is usually less damaging to fall off to the low side (crashing by laying the bike down on the side closest to the ground) than it is to fall to the high side (crashing by flipping the bike and yourself to the high side or the opposite side from the way you were turning). Highsides are one of the worst kinds of crashes you can have on a motorcycle.

Turning safety tips for recreational riders

• Late apex (come into the turn wide) all blind corners so you can see around the turn if someone is coming the other way. When recreational riding on narrow back roads and trails, you should always assume that someone may be coming the other way.

• Slow down before each corner, especially blind turns. Keep your speed low on blind corners so you can accelerate through the turn and take any line you need to avoid someone who might be coming the other way in your lane.

Sand Turns

1 In certain riding areas a natural terrain berm like this small sand dune can be used to help you change direction.

2 In soft terrain like sand it's very important to keep your speed up.

3 To make the turn, shift down and slow by using a little more rear brake.

4 Just before the apex, accelerate hard as you...

5 ...lean it and turn the handlebars slightly.

6 While doing sand turns you can clutch the engine if necessary to keep the RPMs up.

• Pick a good line to follow and stick to it. Many times a crash in a turn can be attributed to missing or not staying on the preferred line. Sometimes it only takes an inch in the wrong direction to make the difference, so it is critical to use the right techniques to help you stick to the preferred line.

Tips to turn around or move your bike when stationary

There are many ways to spin your bike around 180 degrees or move it in any direction while stationary and either sitting on your bike or standing next to it. These are all handy to know and practice because in the right riding or racing situation, it could save you both time and energy.

• Sit on the bike with the engine running in first gear, lean it, rev it, release the clutch, and spin the rear end around and pivot. Called a doughnut for obvious reasons, this technique is good for motocross tracks and sandy desert soil, but not for forest trails where treading lightly is important.

• Sit on the bike in first gear, plant a foot on the ground, clutch it, and wheelie pivot. This is very technical and easier for riders with long legs.

• Stand next to the bike, front brake on, hands on bars, twist the handlebars, and leverage them against the steering stops with your upper body to help spin the rear around.

• Standing next to the bike, drag the rear end around with your left arm on the bars and the right arm on the rear fender or frame grab.

• Standing next to the bike, front brake on and your hands on the bars, use your lower body (hips, leg, and ankle spring) to help you hike the rear end over instead of using your upper body.

Fast Turns

1 If you want to test what you can get away with in turn entrances try what this rider is doing.

2 Take a trusty good handling little bike like this Yamaha TTR125 and enter a turn with a little too much speed and lean angle.

3 You will be surprised how fast you can corner and you will gain a better perspective of what is not enough lean and what is too much!

4 Notice how the rider has his elbow up high as he exits the corner.

- Stop on a hillclimb, dismount, and turn around (see Chapter 7 to find out more about hillclimb extractions).

Advanced turning practice:

- Try turning tighter, faster, and slower, at an early apex, a late apex, and on smoother, rougher, and softer terrain, and so on.
- Try turning 180 degrees and 360 degrees, and set up a figure 8 course.
- Ride over an obstacle (a log, bump, big flat rock, and so on) while turning. The key is to coast over obstacles while turning. Don't be on the gas or brakes or you'll lose traction and do a low side.
- Try turning and leaning the bike enough to slide the front tire, or push it (understeer). This is fun to practice on a damp, high-traction day. Try to push the front tire in the entrance of a turn then powerslide at the exit.
- Set up a short two-cone oval and invite a friend to race around it with you.
- Try trail braking with the rear brake into a turn to make the rear tire slide out to get you set up for the corner.
- See Chapters 16 and 17, which cover brakesliding and powersliding, two advanced turning techniques.
- Try a downhill right-hand turn in soft, rocky, or rutted terrain, as on a steep switchback trail.

Wheelie Turns

1 In certain tight places where you want to turn around quickly you can perform a foot plant turn like this rider is doing. Start by sitting down and a little rearward on the seat with your leg out in the direction you want to turn.

2 With the engine running in first gear, raise the engine rpm and quickly release the clutch, pull back, and a do a wheelie.

3 As it wheelies lean it towards your leg down and be ready to pull the clutch in and stop immediately.

4 Back to earth and aiming the other way.

7 Throttle Control

Good throttle control is essential to conquer technical riding challenges

Throttle control is essential when riding motorcycles or you'll end up like that guy in the movie *On Any Sunday* (a classic must-see motorcycle documentary from 1971) who plowed down his neighbor's mailbox and hedge when he was trying to ride for the first time. That poor sap experienced the classic unintentional, out-of-control acceleration that comes when someone releases the clutch too fast while sitting too far back. The acceleration pulls their body back and turns on the throttle so much they can't shut it off. It is ugly and dangerous. We call it "wrist lock" or "whiskey throttle" and teach how to avoid it by simply sitting forward and leaning forward when releasing the clutch and learning how to coordinate the clutch and throttle to start out. To ride off-road motorcycles, get used to keeping your elbows up and using your wrist to twist the throttle instead of moving your entire arm.

If you're having problems controlling the throttle, especially when riding standing up, you may be putting too much pressure on your right arm and wrist by leaning too far back or by trying to hold yourself up while also working the controls with overstressed arms and hands (also increasing arm pump). The solution is to reposition your body forward so you can carry your upper body weight and steer the bike with your feet and lower body. When accelerating, lean forward slightly and keep your arms bent so you always maintain throttle control. Leaning forward slightly just before twisting the throttle hard also will help you brace yourself and carry the acceleration force with your legs and feet. When sitting, try not to sit too far back or slide back on the seat when accelerating, especially on uphills. Remember: When riding standing up, do not try to hold yourself up with your arms. Doing so will only make the throttle harder to control.

"My riding really improved when I stopped trying to go fast and just concentrated on going forward."

Brian Catterson
Editor-in-Chief, Motorcyclist Magazine

This is a normal hand/wrist grip on the handlebars. The angle may change depending on whether you are sitting or standing, but in this position you will be able to hang on and also operate the throttle and front brake.

This is an overgrip with your hand/wrist grip on the handlebars. In this position you'll be able to give it plenty of throttle, and maybe too much if you're not careful!

This is an undergrip with your hand/wrist grip on the handlebars. In this position you won't overthrottle, but you might sprain your wrist or not be able to give it enough throttle when needed.

Power can both help you and hurt you. With today's high-powered bikes, like the 450cc four-stroke, most people have more power than they know what to do with and they get in trouble because of it. What good is power if you can't control it? The answer is throttle control and sometimes less throttle equals more control. One good example of this is technical hillclimbs where you must keep your wheels in line to stay on line and get to the top. Too much throttle could slew you sideways and miss the preferred line, causing you to shut off the throttle to realign the wheels or to abort the run. Another good example where throttle control is important is a loose sidehill where too much throttle could spin you sideways and spoil a good off-camber traverse and could even cause you to get stuck. It doesn't matter how much horsepower you have, you won't be able to climb a steep technical hill or sidehill if you can't stick to a good line by using a little throttle control.

On the other hand, there are many places, like in sand and mud, where you must be more aggressive with the throttle to keep your momentum moving forward in the power-sapping terrain. The key is knowing when and how much power to apply in each situation, and much of this knowledge simply comes with experience.

Most recreational bikes have engines with smooth and linear power that makes them friendly and easy to control, while racing bikes tend to have harsh and peaky powerbands that are not easy to control. Examples of where throttle control is critical include when you're giving your bike a short, well-timed burst of throttle to generate the speed and traction needed just before climbing a low-traction section of hill. Precise throttle control also comes in handy in slippery situations such as off-camber hill routes, where you must either roll on or roll off the throttle to find traction.

What is happy throttle?

Overactive throttle use, or happy throttle, can make your riding rough or herky-jerky. It usually does little good to twist the throttle back and forth excessively. Young, often hyperactive riders do this and eventually grow out of it. Overuse of the throttle is tiring and the constant sudden acceleration and deceleration will fatigue you prematurely. Old two-stroke engines that didn't idle sometimes required a happy throttle to keep running, but modern smooth-running four-stroke engines don't.

What is short shifting?
What is soft throttle?

Short shifting is when a rider will shift up one gear higher than is needed. Short shifting lowers the engine's rpm and softens the acceleration and deceleration, thus making the ride smoother. Of course, the rider who short shifts will often cover the clutch with two fingers and is ready to "clutch it" or slip the clutch to quickly raise the engine rpm if need be to keep the engine from bogging down. The benefits of short shifting and using a soft throttle in loose, rocky terrain like rock gardens and hillclimbs strewn with rocks is that your rear tire won't spin too much and deflect sideways. Instead, your wheels will stay in line and you'll roll over those loose rocks where maintaining momentum, not stopping and starting, is critical to making it through.

Advanced throttle control practice (some of these can be performed only after reading later chapters):

- Try power sliding around a flat area and be sure to practice both left and right slides. Use the throttle to control how far your rear wheel slides.
- Try climbing a technical hill and picking a more challenging line.
- Try traversing a steep, loose sidehill (off-camber) route and without slipping downhill.

Too much throttle? Not enough? We don't know, but the proper amount of throttle will usually keep you away from situations like this.

- Try riding in rain, mud, snow, or ice where throttle control is critical to staying upright.
- Try a steep hill with low-traction zones where you must roll off and back on the throttle again to stay on line.
- Try a wheelie for a purpose or to show off; either one demonstrates good throttle control.

Just about everything you do on a dirt bike requires precise throttle control, especially while jumping. Where your throttle is at during takeoff has a lot to do with whether the front end will be low, level, or high during the jump.

8 Hillclimbs

Technical hillclimbs require that you pick a good line and stick to it

Climbing hills is one of the most challenging, thrilling things one can do on a dirt bike and something that separates the men from the boys. We have one that we have used for years at MotoVentures and it's nicknamed "The Humbler" because it has it all: it's steep, loose and firm, has turns, ruts, and rocks, and has humbled many good riders. There are many different kinds of hill-climbing challenges out there, so we'll focus on the basics first and then on the two most common technical climbs riders will encounter: long technical hillclimbs and short, low-traction hillclimbs.

Climbing hills is one thing, but getting back down safely after a failed attempt is another. Your ability to get unstuck from a failed hillclimb attempt is one of those critical skills you need to know if you're going to ride off-road.

When performing this exercise you will follow the shape of a giant K to get the bike turned around. So the next time you get stuck climbing a hill, don't panic and don't drop your bike. Just follow these basic procedures for a safe and graceful 180-degree turn back down the hill.

"The secret to climbing hills for your average recreational rider or professional hillclimber is a combination of momentum and clutch control. Gain as much speed as you can early in the climb and continue to carry momentum using plenty of throttle while controlling front-end lift and loss of rpm through fanning of the clutch. See you at the top!"

Kerry Peterson
Five-time World Hillclimb champion, Dirt Rider Magazine's *"Best Hillclimber of All Time"*

How to practice basic hillclimbs

Hillclimbing is one of the trickier things we do on dirt bikes, but once you make it to the top of one, you'll feel like you really accomplished something. On the way up, you'll be concentrating primarily on throttle control, clutch control, gear selection, wheelspin, line selection, and weight transfer.

To practice basic techniques, choose a fairly easy hill with few obstacles and fairly good traction. As with any hillclimb, take a good look at the hill ahead of time and choose what you feel is the easiest, smoothest line. Begin your climb by being back far enough from the base to get the most possible speed that you can safely hit at the start of the hill (this could be as high as third gear). You'll find that momentum is your best friend in hillclimbing, and the more momentum you start out with at the bottom, the easier it will be in the last 25 percent of the hill where most people fail.

Hit the base of the hill in the attack position, carrying as much momentum as possible, and stay on the throttle on the way up. Then, as conditions dictate, you may have to quickly and smoothly shift into a lower gear if you hear the engine start to bog. At some point in nearly every hillclimb, you'll have to shift your weight from the rear to the front to keep the front wheel down as it gets steeper and you get more traction. You can also feather the clutch to keep from wheeling over, as well as using throttle control. The main thing to avoid on a hillclimb is bogging the engine and losing momentum. Once that happens, it's much more difficult to get going again. It's okay to have a good amount of wheelspin on the way up if you're still keeping your momentum moving up the hill.

Now that you've conquered a relatively easy hill several times, you can move to the more difficult climbing scenarios described next.

Long, Loose Hills

1 On long, loose hills it's important to start out with good speed at the bottom and try to maintain it as long as possible.

2 Shift down as you slow down and shift your weight forward to keep your bike from wheeling or shift your weight rearward slightly for more traction.

How to practice long technical hillclimbs

A technical hillclimb may have both loose and firm soil. It usually isn't straight, it might have a vertical ledge or two, and it often has rain ruts running down it. The key to riding technical hills is to stop at the bottom of the hill and read the terrain, looking for traction zones and a good smooth line and then execute it with the right techniques.

To practice technical hillclimbs, locate a long technical uphill, all the better if it has multiple lines that are loose, turning, rutted, and bumpy, requiring that you pick and stick to a good line. Start in first and shift up as you accelerate. Remember, sometimes staying on line is more important than speed, but of course if the hill is long and loose, speed is an important ingredient. Make sure you stand up and ride a little bowlegged or you may fall victim to dreaded butt steer (see page 73). As the hill becomes steeper and more technical you may need to shift down, but try to maintain some speed if you can. Keep leaning forward to keep the front end down, but you may need to move your weight rearward for traction and from side to side to keep the bike on the line you want.

Try not to wheelie too much. This could cause you to shut off the throttle to let the front wheel down to regain control, which could ruin your attempt. Try to keep your wheels in line when driving uphill. Too much throttle could get you sideways and either send you off-line or slow your momentum. If climbing while sitting, do not slide backward on the seat or your bike will wheelie too easily and send you out of control. Look ahead and try to build your speed in the traction zones so you can shut off the throttle or use the clutch and let momentum carry you over the loose patches. Cover the clutch with two fingers in case you need to slip it to keep the revs up or to keep the front wheel down.

Technical Hills

1 To climb a long technical hill it's important to pick and stick to the smoothest, highest traction line possible and attack it with plenty of speed, especially at the bottom.

2 On hills like this there are plenty of rocks and ruts that will turn you if you hit them, so be sure to move your body freely from side to side to keep the bike going where you want it to go.

When following someone and you're both approaching a challenging climb, if you're not sure if the person ahead will make it, drop back and maybe even stop at the bottom to make sure the other rider makes it before you proceed. If you follow someone too closely and they stumble or stall you could get stuck too.

Last, if you can't climb the hill, try not to dig a hole or create a trench. Push with your legs or give it up and turn around to try it again. Again, tread lightly whenever possible and we'll all be better off.

How to practice short, low-traction hillclimbs

Our objective here is to learn a technique that will help you tackle seemingly impossible climbs that lack traction, either from being very steep, very loose, or both. To make things even trickier, in many cases you won't know what's on the top or the other side of hill. This skill will not only get you to the top, but you will also be reducing your impact on the terrain, which is commonly known by respectful off-roaders as *treading lightly*.

To practice low-traction hillclimbs, start by locating a relatively short hill that gets increasingly steeper. Perhaps there's a vertical step at the top, or the top is steep and the soil is loose. Imagine that it has no traction (due to vertical terrain, mud, loose soil, rocks, and so on), and keep in mind the golden rule of climbing up or over a slippery obstacle: Don't try to get traction where there is none. Approach it in second gear (on most bikes) standing up. Accelerate before the hill, getting traction where

Short Climbs

1 To climb a short, steep hill it's important to be very aggressive on your approach by leaning back and accelerating hard to get all your speed and traction before the steepest part where there's little or no traction.

2 At this point you're in the attack position and staying on the gas.

3 Note how the front and rear suspension systems are taxed as you hit the face of the hill. This helps keep the rear wheel driving, too.

4 As your bike climbs almost vertically, lean forward and bend your arms and knees to stay low on the bike. At this point you've got plenty of momentum to make it and can let off the gas.

the traction is, and use momentum instead of relying on traction to carry you through the no-traction zone. Once you know you will make it, using good judgment, shut off the throttle and time your deceleration so you crest the hill at low speed and without spinning the rear tire and leaving a trench. Remember to judge it correctly so you have the momentum for the rear tire to clear the top and then be ready to immediately pull in the clutch and use the brakes in case you must stop or make a tight right or left turn. As you climb over the top, make sure you squat low and absorb the bike to help maintain control. Once the rear tire clears the top you can get back on the throttle and ride away.

What is butt steer?

Sitting while hillclimbing is okay if the approach is smooth, which it rarely is. Sitting down over rough terrain often results in a dirt-bike riding phenomenon we call "butt steer," which is when the rear tire hits a bump or rock and the jolt is transferred through the rider's butt, then torso, and then up to the arms, affecting the steering in a negative way, usually off-line and grinding to a halt nowhere near the top. Standing up will help cure this problem by allowing your legs to absorb and spring with the jolts, giving you better control so you can stay on the best line to climb the hill.

Hillclimbing trivia: Hillclimbing competitions are one of the safest forms of motorcycle competitions and your run is scored by how far up the hill your bike goes, not where your body stops.

5 As you crest stand up and ride away.

6 Hey, short, steep hillclimbs are fun, aren't they?

Advanced hillclimb practice

- Try a hill you can climb and then try a more challenging line.
- Try a challenging hill that has turns, ruts, bumps, no traction, and then full traction and see how you handle it differently.
- Take on a hill with a short approach so your line and acceleration must be perfect.
- Try a really steep hill with a nearly vertical ledge so you must rely on momentum to make it to the top.
- Take on a hill full of rollers with loose rocks everywhere—sounds like fun.
- Try a tall sandy hill or sand dune that requires full power and speed to make it to the top. You'll find that your weight will be more rearward on a sand dune hill than a typical dirt hill.

Rocky Climbs

1 On loose, rocky hillclimbs like this it's hard to keep your bike going straight as your tires "ping pong" off the unstable rocks that litter the hill. On this hill there is the added challenge of negotiating the soft bed of sand the rocks are sitting on.

2 The right amount of speed, careful line selection, and constantly shifting your body position is your best hope of riding over roller rocks like these.

Vertical Banks

1 Some small vertical banks and ledges can be climbed by using the trials roll-up technique of leaning back to wheelie into the face roughly half way up.

2 Then as your bike climbs the steepest part, spring forward with your legs (rapidly transferring your weight forward) to help the rear tire climb up.

3 Presto!

Steep Rock Faces

1 When climbing up steep rock faces be careful not to wheelie or be surprised by sudden acceleration when your spinning rear tire connects with the rock and hooks up or grips the rock.

2 Just lean forward, remain aggressive, and be ready to clutch it or shut off the throttle...

3 ...if it wheelies too much.

How to practice hillclimb extractions

For this exercise you must first simulate getting yourself stuck climbing. Locate a gentle slope and ride straight up it in first gear while sitting down. As you come to a stop, stall the engine on purpose (by not pulling in the clutch) to simulate getting stuck on a hill (leave your bike in gear, as this will help hold it in place during the extraction). As soon as you stop on any hill, hit both brakes hard and try to get the bike stabilized as quickly as possible. Don't pull in the clutch and let it start rolling backward or you'll be in big trouble. After you've stopped, keep the front brake on, put your left foot down, and get off the bike to the left, always holding the front brake on.

Sometimes when you stop on a steep hill you won't be able to keep the bike upright and you may have to lay the bike down, preferably on the left side (away from the throttle—to keep from damaging the throttle tube or filling it with abrasive dirt) to prevent it from sliding downhill. Once under control you might need to wrestle the bike around

Recovering From a Failed Attempt

1 When stopping on a steep hill you may not be able to hold your bike upright, and to stop it from sliding back you will have to lay it down, usually on the left side.

2 To begin to get out of your jam, drag the rear around so the bike is laying across the hill.

3 Next, pick the bike up, always staying on the uphill side.

4 Keeping the front brake on, go ahead and hop on and ride it down. There's no need to start the engine at this point, but you can bumpstart it as you head for the bottom.

90 degrees by dragging either end, usually the rear, with your right hand while holding the handlebars with your left hand. The bike will then be perpendicular to the hill so you can lift it up again without it rolling down.

Keep in mind that whenever stopping on a hill only put your foot down on the uphill side of the bike, never on the downhill side of the bike. Now, with both the front brake and gearbox keeping the wheels from rolling and holding you in place and with the bike standing up, lean it into your hip, turn the handlebars full left, pull the clutch in, release the front brake pressure, and the bike will slowly roll backward. At that point, you can usually control your backward speed with the front brake. When it rolls backward, walk with it, curving it left to stop parallel to the hill with you standing on the uphill side of the bike. Keep holding the front brake on and "wiggle walk" the front wheel by turning the handlebars full left and full right repeatedly to "walk" the front end around to where it is pointing almost straight downhill.

At this point you can remount, but make sure to place your downhill foot on the footpeg. Never put your foot down on the downhill side of the bike; if you do, you'll greatly increase your

Turning Around After Getting Stuck

1 To simulate getting stuck on a hill with the bike upright, stall your engine by stopping without pulling in the clutch (to prevent you from rolling backward).

2 Dismount, lean the bike into your hip, turn the handlebars, release the clutch, and control the bike as you slowly back it down with the front brake.

3 Walk back with the bike and "wiggle walk" the front wheel around...

4 ...until you're pointing downhill.

5 Get ready to mount up and place your foot on the downhill foot peg.

6 Avoid losing your balance at this critical time. Pull in the clutch and release the brakes and begin rolling downhill.

chances of losing your balance and crashing downhill (crashing downhill can easily hurt both the bike and the rider). When performing a hillclimb extraction, don't be in a hurry, take your time. It would be silly to crash and hurt yourself or the bike while simply trying to get back down a hill.

Sometimes after a failed hillclimb, the hill is too steep (or the rider is too tired) to safely ride down. In that case you may want to "bulldog" the bike down (see the next chapter for how to bulldog down a hill).

Advanced hillclimb extraction practice

- Try a hillclimb extraction on a steeper hill where you can't stop standing up or you'll slide rearward, a hill where you must lay the bike down and drag it around with your arms.
- Try a hillclimb extraction on a loose hill where everything's sliding.
- Try a hillclimb extraction from the right side of the bike in case you need to someday.
- Try a hillclimb extraction from a steep single-track trail.
- Try a hillclimb extraction on a hill with massive ruts in it.

9 Downhills

Get good with the front brake and you will fear no downhill

Probably the most intimidating obstacle for most new riders are steep downhills. They are scary just to look at, much less ride. What most riders worry about is controlling their speed on the way down. The trick of course is precise braking and body position, along with picking a good line and *taking your time.*

How to practice downhills

To practice riding downhill, locate a short, challenging, yet rideable hill. You may even walk it at first so you know exactly where you want to go. Begin your descent as slowly as possible in first gear, but not so slow to be unstable and lose your balance. Approach the downhill at a 90-degree angle and steadily follow your line to the edge, knowing it will take you down the line you walked. As you start down a steep hill, pull in the clutch, apply both brakes, and shift your weight rearward, almost as far as you can, to help keep your rear tire on the ground. Too much front brake, or not enough weight over the rear tire, and you'll find yourself flipping over the front end, which could also happen if the tire gets stuck in a hole or against a rock. So be careful with the front brake on steep hills. Apply the rear brake almost to the point of skidding to go as slow as possible.

"Riders seem to be very brave on steep downhills until they have a reason not to be brave. One bad experience can instill a healthy amount of cowardice. Remember that the traction and soil composition of a downhill are much more important than the angle. If the soil is loose, it's much easier to stop, but it's also easier to knife the front end. Hard-pack soil gives you much more confidence initially, but when it's time to slow down, you need more space and use gentle braking. Either way, the run-off at the bottom is very important. Looking at all these things is critical before you take that leap."

Ron Lawson
Dirt Bike Magazine *editor since 1990*

On gradual downhills at modest speeds, engine braking with the bike in a lower gear will suffice, but on steep downhills, where you must go even slower, you will have to be in first gear, pull in the clutch to keep the engine running, and control your speed entirely with your brakes. If you stall your engine, don't worry. You don't need it at this point. Simply continue to coast down to where you can start it up again.

Control your speed on downhills and don't let it build up too much. Remember to carefully pick your line and stay on it by leaning the bike left or right (steering it). Sometimes it can be tricky when you must either avoid a rut or stay in one while descending. On extremely steep or loose sections of a downhill you may need to let off one or both brakes to maintain control and resume braking in firmer terrain farther down the hill. If it is too steep (or rutted) and you can't keep your foot on the rear brake you can purposely stall the engine in gear and use the clutch. This will act a little like a rear brake to help you control your speed.

Caution: Steep downhills can be a one-way trip if you're not careful. When you come to a steep downhill you need

Steep Downhills

1 Approach a steep downhill like this straight on, in first gear. To ride slow enough and to prevent your engine from stalling, you must pull in the clutch and rely entirely on your brakes.

2 As you start down, very slowly lean rearward and keep your speed in check with both brakes, primarily the front brake except where it's too soft or loose.

3 This is the scary point. Simply keep the front wheel straight, your weight over the rear, and as much brakes as your bike can handle without flipping forward.

4 You made it!!

to ask yourself if you're sure the road or trail ahead takes you where you want to go. Are you good enough to climb back up the hill you just went down? If the road or trail at the bottom dead-ends or is impassable, you may have to climb that hill to get back. (Yikes!)

What is bulldogging?

Bulldogging is a classic time-tested technique that you may need to use someday to go down a hill that is too steep to ride down. To bulldog your bike down a hill, you must dismount and walk down the hill alongside your bike, bulldogging it as you go. To do this, grab the bike by the horns (handlebars) from the left side and put your feet out in front, next to the front wheel. Lean back into the hill and let your right armpit settle around the area where the gas tank meets the front of the seat with the bike leaning over into the right side of your torso. Then, walk it down slowly, applying the front brake to keep your speed in check. On really steep, loose hills, you can leave the bike in gear and use the clutch to release the rear wheel when needed. If the bike starts getting out of control, just let it go and sit down. With any luck, you'll both be stopping soon.

Bulldogging is actually a rodeo term where cowboys wrestle steers to the ground by wrapping their arms around the animals' horns and pulling to the back and side. You can try to ride down a steep hill, but with the long travel suspension of today's off-road bikes, the geometry changes too much when the forks compress on steep downhills, which will make you want to flip forward

and crash forward or *endo* (short for end-over-end). Bulldogging your bike will allow you to safely descend a steep hill if you can't ride down it. Sometimes when it gets this steep it's better to swallow your pride and just bulldog it down.

What is a drop-off?

A drop-off is an advanced off-road riding technique where on a steep downhill you may encounter a vertical drop that may be short enough to ride down, or it may not. If it is short enough to ride, treat it like any steep downhill where you need to shift your weight even farther back. If it is not short enough to ride down, you may be able to jump downhill (very advanced). Approach it slowly and gently wheelie, or float, the front tire off the edge of the drop-off and try to land with the front tire first. Immediately continue braking, hopefully with enough space to maintain control. By combining great wheelie and braking skills you will have the confidence to take alternative lines like drop-offs.

What is bump starting?

Bump starting is a convenient way for you to start your bike on a downhill. To bump start your bike, point it downhill and put it in second or third gear to let the engine turn over easier. Pull in the clutch and start rolling. After picking up a little speed, let the clutch out. This will turn over the engine and start the bike. You can also bump start a bike by pulling it (or pushing it) by various means, but this is only recommended as a last resort by expert riders.

On soft or loose downhills don't try to go too slow; let it roll, pick your lines very carefully, try not to turn too much, and use the rear brake a little more.

If you're unable to ride down a steep hill you can always bulldog your bike down it by killing the engine, but keeping it in gear and walking alongside it using the front brake and the clutch as a rear brake.

Advanced downhill practice

- Try steeper downhills.
- Try a steep and loose downhill.
- Try changing lines on steep hills.
- Try a downhill with ruts in it.
- Try rolling off or jumping off a small downhill drop-off or vertical descent.
- Try a hill that is so steep you have to bulldog your bike down it.
- Try a steep downhill right-hand turn that is also loose and rutted. This tough combination is especially challenging for right-handed people who have not yet learned how to carefully use their brakes or counterbalance.

Dropoffs

1 Some steep dropoffs you can ride down, others you must jump off.

2 Approach the drop at a 90-degree angle and lean back as you descend, momentarily releasing the front brake at the steepest point.

Tales from the Trail:
ONE MAN'S SOLUTION TO A STEEP AND LOOSE HILL

When riding in remote canyons with steep hills always take the time and make sure the hill you want to descend isn't too steep or loose for you to climb back out or you could end up like a friend who got temporarily stuck in one. He had to leave his bike behind and hike for hours back to his truck, where he drove home. The next day, he purchased a paddle tire for the rear. He then drove back, hiked for hours back in, mounted the paddle tire, and was finally able to ride his bike back out. Believe it. There are plenty of unclimbable hills out there, even for the best riders.

Rain Ruts

1 Whenever learning or teaching how to ride down a steep rain-rutted hill like this it's a good idea to look it over carefully, maybe even walk it like a trials rider would in a section to locate exactly where you want to go.

2 When tackling downhill ruts, stand up and lean rearward as you descend and stay on the correct line and out of those ruts by leaning the bike and turning the handlebars to steer. Keep it slow!

Rock Ledges

1 Some steep dropoffs like this you can jump off and land rear tire first, just make sure there is enough traction to float a wheelie off the top and...

2 ...enough room to land and slow down at the bottom.

10 Hillside Turns and Sidehills

Use weight transfer and momentum to navigate these tricky obstacles

Making a turn on a hill is a simple yet important skill to master. It combines the physics of riding up a hill, turning on that hill, and riding down it. When making a hillside turn you must keep in mind that your bike has a limited amount of steering radius, so it's important to always follow an arc. If you try to turn too tight, run into the steering lock, and can't turn it anymore, you'll lose your balance at the absolute worst place and your simple U-turn on a hill can result in a painful and embarrassing downhill fall.

Riding a trail on the side of a hill, especially a loose one, can be challenging if you don't know what techniques to employ (sidehills are also known as off-cambers). For body position, you can ride them sitting down, but you won't be able to control the bike as much as if you tackle it standing up. In many cases, standing up will be the only chance you have of making it across.

Riding sidehills also requires careful terrain reading, line selection, throttle control, and proper weight distribution. If you hit a loose section your bike will start slipping down the hill and too much throttle will spin your rear wheel and make it even worse. Without proper weight distribution there's no hope at all. Treat every sidehill with the following techniques and a little respect and you'll have the best chance at traversing them.

"At the Erzberg Rodeo (annual extreme enduro in Austria) I was passed by a rider with obvious trials skills who was able to use a line through a rocky sidehill I didn't even see. Riding trials has really opened up my sidehill line options."

Cory Graffunder

Finished 4th in the 2011 AMA National Endurocross Series, finished 3rd Overall in three events, and raced the famous Erzberg Enduro three times finishing 18th, 6th, and 5th.

How to practice hillside turns

To practice a turn on a hill, locate an unobstructed, gently sloping dirt hill. Think of the hill in three parts that need to be run together: an uphill, a turn, and a downhill. Approach the hill standing up in second gear. Lean forward, and with a burst of throttle, accelerate aggressively and generate all the traction and speed needed to get you up the hill and around the turn. On your approach, once you know you have the speed to make it (using good judgment), shut off the throttle and allow the bike to decelerate (don't pull in the clutch) as you round the top of the turn following a wide arc (to the left at first, then to the right). It is important that you follow an arc and not try to turn too sharply. For your body position, simply counterbalance, just as you would in a flat turn, but much more so. You'll lean the bike into the turn (downhill) and counterbalance with your body opposite of the turn (uphill). Finally, as you round the top of your turn and start downhill, shift your weight rearward and start to apply the brakes to control your downhill speed. This exercise may seem simple, but hillside turns are often underestimated, especially by new riders, and can deliver a damaging downhill crash.

Hillside Turns

1 Hillside turns require that you aggressively charge up a hill and with enough speed to carry you around the turn.

2 As you near the apex of the turn, shut off the throttle, ...

3 ...follow a gradual arc as you turn, ...

4 ...and counterbalance the same way you would on flat ground.

5 Sidehill turns are a bit intimidating since a simple fall could end up being more painful if you fall on the downhill side.

6 Now that wasn't so tough now, was it?

Advanced hillside turn practice:

- Try a hillside turn on a steeper hill.
- Try a tighter radius hillside turn.
- Try a hillside turn on loose hill.

- Try a hillside turn at different speeds.
- Try a hillside turn with a log to ride over in the middle to combine three things: turning, hills, and wheelies.

Big Hillside Turns

1 It is fun to practice on a big hillside turn like this.

2 Approach it aggressively and use good judgment to make sure...

3 ...you have enough speed to get up the hill *and* around the corner.

4 Turning on sidehills isn't just for fun, as many technical trails feature these types of turns as a way of avoiding big obstacles.

How to practice riding sidehills

Locate a gentle, firm, smooth dirt sidehill. Ride it standing up in first or second gear. A little speed is good, especially if it's loose. Be smooth and steady with the throttle and try to keep your wheels in line. In a situation like this you can "short shift" your bike, which is when you shift up one more gear than is optimum to lower the engine rpm and smooth out the power delivery to help keep your wheels in line. Also, try to gently roll on or roll off the throttle so you don't break the rear tire loose. You can also slip the clutch (with two fingers) and even drag the rear brake a little to help keep the rear tire from spinning and skewing you sideways on the hill.

To counter the slope, keep your balance, and fight for traction, you must position your body in the middle of the bike, not too forward or rearward. It will also feel like you're leaning the bike into the hill, but you're countering that lean by shifting your hips to the downhill side of the bike so you can pressurize the downhill footpeg, which will drive the tires into the sidehill and bite, getting as much traction as possible. Be sure to practice traversing both to the left and right, and shift your body the other way when you do. When sidehilling on really loose terrain, plan your route to include a gradual loss of elevation, especially above places where there is no way out.

Sidehills

1 Riding sidehills can be tricky, especially if the sidehill is loose or if you are trying to follow a narrow path.

2 Use a smooth and steady throttle control to keep from spinning the rear tire, carry some speed if it's loose, and steer your bike to keep it on line by leaning it instead of turning your handlebars.

3 To get traction, shift your weight (hips) to the downhill foot peg, which will help drive your tires into the hill.

4 Some of the toughest, most famous dirt bike trails in the country feature lots of tricky sidehill sections.

Slippery Sidehills

1 Narrow sidehill trails are often the first place riders realize they have the ability to stay on line, or not.

2 In this case, the rider suddenly turned up the hill, shifted his weight to the center, and hit the throttle, causing his bike to spin out and...

3 ...and begin to go out of control.

4 If you slide off the downhill side of an extremely steep sidehill trail, it may take you hours to get your bike back up and on the trail again.

Single-track riding practice begins with riding sidehills

This is the first exercise in our curriculum that really tests your ability to stay on line and ride a single-track trail. In popular OHV riding areas, a sidehill route could be on any rideable hillside (please remember to tread lightly), allowing you to climb or descend at will, but in off-road and dual-sport riding there is usually a narrow path or single-track trail you must follow and stay on. Single-track has always been a favorite of mountain bike and technical off-road riders. The problem is it is hard to find a novice-level single track. It usually takes intermediate and advanced skills. To develop your single-track riding skills, practice this sidehill exercise and our slalom and board-ride exercises (see next chapter).

Single-track trivia: In the early days of off-road riding in America, riders would follow the perfectly rideable paths made by cows and other large wildlife. Naturally, they called this cow-trailing back then. Today, many single-track trails are now the back-country highways for both wildlife and humans.

Advanced sidehill practice:

- Try steeper, looser sidehills and see how well you can stay stuck to the side of the hill.
- Try sidehilling on solid rock with great traction.
- Try changing lines farther up or down a sidehill.
- Try rocky, loose sidehills.
- Try riding a challenging sidehill faster and then slower.
- Try making a tight turn uphill or downhill from a sidehill.

11 Steering While Standing Up

Steer with your legs and feet to stay on line

Steering your bike by using your legs and feet while riding standing up is a very efficient way to ride. This exercise is great practice for riding hillclimbs, sand washes, single track, and ruts.

When riding standing up at midspeed, the correct way to steer an off-road bike is with your feet and legs. Usually the terrain is bumpy where we ride, and that requires standing up. One of the tricks to riding standing up is positioning your body weight over your legs and feet, and in this position, you can also steer the bike with your lower body. In this position, it is easy to put pressure on one footpeg or another and create a lean to the left or right, causing your bike to turn almost effortlessly.

Even though it might seem to be the opposite, by standing on the footpegs, you will have a lower center of mass for you and your bike than if you were sitting on the seat. Steering the bike with your lower body will allow you to ride harder and longer and will give you the ability to ride more confidently in technical sections such as sand washes, hillclimbs, sand dunes, and muddy areas—anywhere you need to maintain speed and turn while standing or anywhere you need to stay on a narrow line.

"My advantage when I ride and race off-road is I stand up as often as possible. It may seem like it requires more energy; however, when I position my body correctly I can use my lower body to help turn the bike, spring for jumps, and absorb impacts, and at the end of the day still have a significant amount of energy left. Here in the northeastern part of America where it is very technical you must constantly ride standing up so your ability to steer with your lower body is critical."

Fred Hoess

16-Time ISDE Gold Medalist and multi-time Top American, numerous AMA National Enduro and Hare Scrambles victories

How to practice steering while standing up

Slalom exercise: To practice steering with your legs, use a five-traffic-cone slalom exercise laid out on a smooth, dirt straight with a fairly hardpacked surface. Use full-size cones so you'll hit them if you don't ride around them. Set up your cones in a straight line approximately 12 paces apart. While riding standing up with your weight forward over the bars, approach the slalom in second or third gear. Decide which side of the first cone you will go around. As you round that cone, lean your bike in the direction of the turn and counterbalance your body in the other direction. As you proceed to the next cone, you must shift the bike's lean to the other direction while shifting your body the opposite way to counterbalance. At speed, you will not turn the handlebars, just lean the bike left and right.

For this exercise, it helps to ride a little bowlegged and let the bike float between your legs and lean from inside of one leg to the inside of the other. At first, you'll just weave through the slalom course, concentrating on getting your

Steering While Standing

1 Riding through a slalom course will help you experience steering with your feet and legs and prepare you for sand washes.

2 Approach the first slalom cone standing up at a modest speed and lean the bike in the direction of the turn while shifting your hip and outside leg in the opposite direction.

3 Swap these positions to go around each cone. Next, speed up and try to steer more by shifting your weight, not by turning your handlebars.

body position correct for each cone. As you get more comfortable, speed up and try to go through the slalom at a shallower angle. The faster you go, the more shallow the angle will be and the quicker you must shift from left to right. You know you're going too fast if you start hitting the cones. Be quick with your transitions, proactive not reactive, and don't get behind. Remember, do not lean rearward; instead, move your body from side to side, keeping your weight forward on the machine. Leaning rearward will tire out your upper body. Steering with your legs is easy to perform but sometimes hard to feel, especially on slippery days.

To get a feel for what it's like to steer the bike with your legs, it is best to practice it on days when the traction is high, like just after some rain has soaked into the ground. Concentrate on pressuring each footpeg to create the bike's lean angles. Steering with your legs properly is a lot like snow skiing properly—you'll know when you're doing it right and when you're not.

Narrow Paths

1 To stay on this narrow six-inch board, ride standing up in first gear, stay as centered as possible, and instead of turning the handlebars to steer it you must rely on leaning it slightly to the right or left.

2 If your front tire comes off the board don't try to get it back on from the side, just ride off and turn around and try it again.

3 Keep your speed slow so if your front tire comes off the board and starts skidding against it, you can stop quickly and put your foot down to save it.

Board-ride exercise: Another way to practice steering with your legs is to use a 20-foot (or longer), 6-inch-wide plank of wood. The obvious object with this exercise is to ride the entire length of it without coming off. For this exercise, stay in first gear, and if you miss the end of the board or your tires come off the board, don't try to get back on, just turn around and try it again. This exercise really shows who can stay on line and who can't and can be very frustrating for some. People who are used to steering their bikes primarily with the handlebars and have not yet learned how to steer by leaning usually have a hard time with this exercise. However, it is a lot better to learn what you need to practice in an exercise like this board ride than in the back country on a tough single-track trail next to a cliff.

Advanced practice for steering while standing up:
- Try coasting down a smooth, gradual hill at more than a walking speed while standing up, take your hands off the handlebars, and try steering with your feet, just like you would do on your bicycle.

Advanced Standing Practice

1 A fun way to practice steering your bike with your lower body while standing up is to locate a smooth downhill road like this one and place some markers on it to steer around.

2 Start by picking up a little speed with the bike in second gear, then release the throttle and gradually decelerate as you stand up and perform this unique slalom exercise.

3 To steer it you may have to press your legs against the bike, and of course always be ready to grab the handlebars if you feel out of control.

- Try riding through the slalom faster or stagger the cones for more turning.
- Try this exercise on a day when the ground has great traction and you can ride faster to really feel the benefits of steering with your legs.
- Try riding down the bottom center of a long rain rut without scrubbing the sides.

- Try riding more technical hillclimbs, sand washes, and more challenging single-track trails.
- Try riding down a deep sand wash and sticking to a straighter line as opposed to constantly turning. You'll actually find that you'll be using lots of body English to keep the bike going in a straight line.

Standing on the Trail

1 Let's take what we learned in the cone exercise out to the trail.

2 Riding sand successfully requires maintaining the right amount of speed, keeping your weight back so the front tire doesn't dig in, ...

3 ...keeping the handlebars straight and steering by leaning the bike gently to the right or left just like in the 5-cone slalom exercise.

4 Don't forget to keep the front end light on loose trails like this.

12 Wheelies

Wheelies are fun, impressive, and can be very practical too

A wheelie is what happens when you accelerate quickly and the front wheel lifts off the ground. "Wheelieing" for a purpose is a practical skill that everyone who rides off-road should practice and perfect. In this chapter, we learn and practice how to "pop a wheelie" for a purpose *and* for fun.

Learning how to wheelie will help you develop good throttle control and rear brake feel. There are many times out on the trail where popping the front wheel over an obstacle is the best way to tackle that section. Crossing over logs, ruts, holes, and puddles are just a few examples. Wheelies are also critical for popping up and over small, steep ledges, as well as setting up your bike to jump off a steep dropoff. After a few seasons in the saddle, dirt bikers usually figure out all sorts of situations where it is best to wheelie the front tire over something rather than plow into it. Good wheelie skills really open up your line options.

At MotoVentures we use two wheelie practice exercises: (1) wheelies for a purpose, performed in the standing, attack position, and (2) extended wheelies for fun, performed sitting down.

How to practice wheelies for a purpose

To practice a wheelie for a purpose, start by locating an approximately 12-inch-diameter log and bury it slightly so it won't roll when you ride over it (or find a similar obstacle already on the trail). Approach the log at a 90-degree angle, in first gear, standing up in the attack position. At approximately 2 feet before the log, blip the throttle (hit the throttle quickly for a short time) and pull back slightly on the handlebars. That's what we call the blip-distance. As soon as the front

"When approaching a log or pole that I must wheelie over I first compress my suspension with my legs right before the obstacle so that it is fully extended and I have all my suspension to soak up the obstacle so I can avoid getting kicked by it and so I get back on the throttle sooner."

Cory Graffunder
Finished 4th in 2011 AMA National Endurocross Series, finished 3rd Overall in three events, and raced the famous Erzberg Rodeo three times finishing 18th, 6th, and 5th

end goes over the log, shut off the throttle before the rear tire hits the log and let it decelerate over the log. Be sure to absorb the bump with your legs when the rear tire rolls over it. If the log rolls when you ride over it, you are probably not shutting the throttle off soon enough. You can accelerate away after the rear tire clears the log.

Once you get the correct throttle blip-distance timing, then you must learn to coordinate and time your throttle blip with a leg and arm spring to help lift the front tire. To do this, as you approach the point where you blip the throttle, remember to first quickly shift your weight downward primarily with your legs. This will compress your suspension. As your suspension and legs and arms rebound, try to coordinate that upward movement with a well-timed throttle blip. Performed correctly, the front wheel will come off the ground easily. This technique requires coordinated body movements and weight shifting (leg spring), not speed, not a big burst of throttle, and not a hard pull back on the handlebars.

Also, be careful not to overgrip your hand on the throttle for this exercise. Overgripping is when you shift your hand forward so you can twist your wrist even more to open the throttle. It's harder to control a throttle with an overgrip, and with this grip if the bike suddenly hooks up you could easily give it too much throttle and lose control.

Using your suspension to help wheelie is a valuable technical skill that can be handy when traction is minimal. Start with small objects to practice on, then gradually take on larger objects as your skills improve. Remember, active legs and good throttle timing is the key to performing a good wheelie for a purpose.

Obstacle Wheelie

1 To practice a wheelie for a purpose for the first time, locate an object like this small log.

2 Approach it at a 90-degree angle, riding standing up in first gear, and blip the throttle about 18 inches before the object.

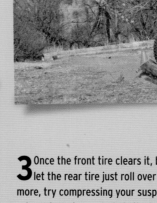

3 Once the front tire clears it, be sure to shut off the throttle and let the rear tire just roll over it. If you want to help the bike more, try compressing your suspension before the object and when it rebounds spring up to help it wheelie.

How to practice wheelies for fun

To practice wheelies for fun, find an unobstructed dirt (no pavement for practicing!) straightaway and a bike with a friendly powerband (like a four-stroke) and a good rear brake. There are two types of fun wheelies you can practice: balance wheelies and power wheelies. If your bike has enough power and accelerates quickly, most people can perform a power wheelie, but performing a balance wheelie requires some training, lots of experience, and strong nerves. Balance wheelies are more impressive than power wheelies, and riding one for a distance demonstrates great throttle and brake control. Dirt bikes are the best tool for the job of learning any kind of motorcycle wheelie techniques.

To practice a balance wheelie, start out by sitting near the rear of the seat, pick up a little speed, and shift into second. To get the front wheel up, as you gradually accelerate in second gear, quickly pull in the clutch (with two fingers) to increase the engine rpm, then release the clutch quickly (flick it) while pulling back on the handlebars to help get the front end up. As the front end rises and you accelerate, be sure to cover the rear brake with your right foot and be prepared to shut off the throttle and apply the rear brake as it gets higher. Each time you wheelie, gradually let the front end get higher and start using the rear brake more to control the height and help you bring it back down to earth. (You'll soon find it only takes a tap of the rear brake. Slamming on the rear brake will make for a really hard landing.)

There is a sweet spot on every motorcycle that we call the balance point where the angle of the wheelie is just right, so that it feels like it is almost balancing on its own. Once

The trick to riding a balance wheelie is using your rear brake to keep from going over backward. Start by sitting down, and as you accelerate through second gear "clutch it" to pop your wheelie, and as you speed up, shift up into a higher gear. You can keep it in that "balance window" by subtly alternating between the throttle and rear brake.

Tales from the Trail:
SHOWING OFF CAN BACKFIRE

One Easter weekend our family was gathering at our favorite riding area known as "the tree" in the desert just outside of Phoenix. When we got there we formed our pits and set up shade and seating for everyone to hang out and barbecue. At the time, I was racing motocross on a sponsored 1974 Husqvarna CR400 and was feeling pretty good about myself and my newest riding stunt, wheelies. With everyone watching, I wheelied back and forth, riding longer and longer wheelies each time. On the last pass the bike bogged so I gave it more (too much) throttle, and when it hit the powerband, I looped out, dismounting unceremoniously off the back of the bike going at least 45 miles per hour. I tried to run and got in a few strides before flipping end over end, just like my bike was doing. We both survived and my family was impressed, especially my brothers who couldn't stop laughing and wouldn't let me live it down for years. From that day on I learned to use the rear brake when doing wheelies and have *never* been over backward since.

you get it high enough to hit the balance point, simply alternate between the throttle and brake to keep it in that balance window. Once you get the hang of it, you'll find that the smoother and more subtle you are with the throttle and rear brake, the easier it is to keep the bike angled in that narrow balance window.

You also use your body position to keep it in the balance point as well. Once the front end is in the air, your body will pivot forward while your butt is still back at the rear of the seat, with your chest and helmet closer to the gas tank (peek around the tank to see where you are going). Move your arms to pivot your torso back and forth to help keep the bike in the sweet spot.

Power wheelies are faster than a wheelie for a purpose because they can be performed in a higher gear than first, but shorter in length. Power wheelies are much easier to perform, especially if you have a bike with abundant power.

Take learning how to balance wheelie step by step to gradually build your confidence, with each pass developing the faith that the rear brake is a fail-safe to keep you from going over backward. With practice you can ride along an almost vertical wheelie by using the rear brake and throttle to keep it up while upshifting and accelerating through the gears; but with a balance wheelie, you don't have to go fast to keep it up. That's the impressive part. With enough room, a good rider can keep the front wheel up so long it will eventually stop rolling and lose its gyroscopic effect. This will make it much harder to maintain a wheelie and will result in a harder landing when the nonspinning front tire hits the ground at speed.

What is a nose wheelie?

A nose wheelie is an advanced technique where a rider picks up a little speed, pulls in the clutch, closes the throttle, and firmly applies the front brake. This slows the bike suddenly and,

Basic Wheelie

1 The easiest way to pop a wheelie is to begin by rolling in first or second gear.

2 Momentarily pull in the clutch slightly to raise the engine revs and then release the clutch quickly.

3 The next trick is to accelerate and wheelie higher up to, but not beyond, the balance point.

4 The only way to learn how to perform a balance wheelie like this is to try it over and over again and gradually increase your feel, judgment, and confidence.

5 You must train your brain that the rear brake will save you from going over backward and the throttle will help you keep it up in the balance window.

6 And back on two wheels. Don't ever slam the rear brake to come back down, as the landing could end up being pretty harsh.

coupled with a little weight transfer to the front, causes the rear end to rise in the air and stay there for a distance until coming to a stop and dropping back down. Having this ability is really fun and impressive and demonstrates tremendous front brake feel and the ability to operate on the threshold of lock up. On the right bike and surface an experienced rider can ride a nose wheelie for a good distance before setting the rear tire down.

To practice a nose wheelie, locate a flat—or better yet, gradual—downhill that has great traction. As you carefully apply the front brake and the front tire slows, unload the rear suspension gently by transferring your weight forward and up to help get the rear tire off the ground. From there, it's just a matter of how brave you are as you progressively work up to the balance point, much like when you are learning how to ride a balance wheelie. Of course, the dangerous part of doing a nose wheelie is squeezing too hard and locking up the front tire, which will vault you forward over the handlebars (aka, endo or face plant).

The bottom line once again is if you want to learn this skill it is *much* better to learn it on

Nose wheelies demonstrate incredible front brake control.

a small, lightweight dirt bike or trials bike, in the dirt, than on *any* other motorcycle in *any* other environment.

What is a bunny hop?

A bunny hop is a very advanced off-road riding technique where a rider can ride over an obstacle and not touch it with either tire. To perform a bunny hop, a rider simply does a wheelie over a small obstacle, and before the rear wheel hits it and the front wheel comes down, the rider abruptly shuts off the throttle and transfers his or her body weight forward or upward by quickly springing with his or her legs. With the correctly timed leg spring, weight transfer, and suspension rebound, a rider can hop the rear tire off the ground and clear small obstacles without even touching them.

This technique is great for trials for sure, but off-roaders with this skill will have a real advantage with great rear wheel awareness, which will come in handy for tricky

Bunny Hop

1 A bunny hop is an advanced technique that comes in handy in certain situations like riding over a ditch, rock, log, or rain rut. Start by riding standing up in second gear, and as you approach, first quickly bend at your knees and arms downward to compress your suspension.

2 As it rebounds, pull back on the handlebars and wheelie, and as the front wheel rises high enough, quickly shut off the throttle and spring with your legs up and forward.

3 Time your wheelie, rapid deceleration, and weight shifting and you will be surprised what you can "bunny hop" with this technique.

4 Where did the bunny hop originally come from? BMX freestylers.

climbs and slippery ledges. Here again, a bunny hop is much easier to learn on a trials bike or lightweight dirt bike than any other motorcycle.

Advanced wheelie practice:
- Try to wheelie over bigger logs, with slipperier approaches.

- Practice both power wheelies and balance wheelies.
- Try longer wheelies where you have to shift gears.
- Try a foot-plant wheelie to turn around in a tight space.
- Try a nose wheelie while riding down a steep hill with good traction.
- Try a bunny hop over a rain rut or over a small object like an empty water bottle.

Water Crossing Wheelie

1 Some short and shallow water crossings can be wheelied across, but use caution and be ready for the drag on the rear wheel in the water to make it hard to maintain that wheelie.

2 Dropping your front wheel down prematurely when wheelying across water could result in a crash.

3 You can see the front wheel starting to come down now.

4 Even though there's lots of water spraying around in the photo, the rider and the airbox area of the bike are actually staying dry.

13 Whoops

Riding whoops is fun and thrilling, but very exhausting!

Whoops are when the surface of the track, trail, or road has bumps of similar sizes with peaks and valleys that cause your body and suspension to get a great workout. Some riders don't like trails with a lot of whoops (short for the term *whoop-de-do*), while others love the challenge and thrill of trying to take them fast. Considering the fact that you'll run into whoops at some point on just about every trail, you might as well get used to them and learn to ride them correctly.

Whoops can be either manmade, like those on a motocross track, or formed naturally from long travel off-road vehicle suspensions moving up and down, loading and unloading the rear tire, causing it to spin and move soil each time it comes back down.

Most whoop sections are usually ridden at speed and require a standing up "attack stance"—sitting through whoops is only possible if you take them slow. Whoops come in many shapes and sizes and can be formed in either dirt or sand. Giant desert whoops formed by off-road racing trucks with much more wheel travel than motorcycles can be really challenging, and because of the high speeds, can be really dangerous too. All whoops demand your attention, sap your strength, and will test your bike's suspension. Before practicing whoops, make sure you are fit and take some time to make sure your suspension is set up correctly and functioning properly (see the information on bike preparation in Chapter 21).

"You need both speed and strength to ride good in a whoop section. Try your best to hit the tops of the whoops to keep your speed up using your arms and legs to keep getting traction. The more effort you put out in the whoops the better your results will be."

Jonah Street
Three-Time Baja 500 winner, Best in the Desert and SCORE Series champion, finished Paris to Dakar three times, winner of two stages

How to practice whoops

To practice whoops, first you have to find some. A local practice or homemade motocross track should have some, as well as just about any desert trail. You can typically find whoops on wooded trails, especially if there's a straight, sandy section where riders have been gassing it hard or braking hard (forming braking bumps).

Tackling whoops at a good clip requires fitness, strength, timing, judgment, technique, confidence, and a lot of experience. One of the problems with whoops is that you either need to take them slowly and safely or click it up a gear and blaze through them relatively quickly. To take big whoops at a medium speed feels awkward and will sap your energy in a flash.

In fact, whoops are best ridden while accelerating, but that also accelerates the speed at which things can go wrong.

When riding through whoops at speed, ultimately the goal is to have your wheels bounce and skip across the tops and not fall into the bottoms, especially the front end. This requires some speed and bravery. Shift up, pick up your speed, shift your weight rearward, keep the throttle on and spring and absorb with your legs as much as you can. The bike will actually pivot underneath you, like a teeter-totter, as you strive to keep your body centered over the bike, using lots of back-and-forth motions with your arms, and up-and-down motions with your legs. This is a time where you may want to grip the tank occasionally with your knees to help control and stabilize the bike.

Once you feel comfortable taking whoops with some speed, you can use the first whoop to jump into a whoop section and clear several whoops at once, and you can use them to jump out again, clearing even more. Try to pick the smoothest line through whoop sections, and

Basic Whoops

1 Attack motocross whoop sections aggressively by shifting up a gear, accelerating and wheelying through them, being careful to not let your front wheel drop into the bottoms.

2 If your front wheel does come down in a whoop section you can use the next whoop to jump several whoops and pick up your rhythm again.

3 Riding whoops requires great arm and leg strength.

you can either try to jump into the whoop section doubling and tripling the first few, then try to create a rhythm of doubling your way through the rest, but most often with whoop sections you end up just pounding through them as fast as you can.

Professional racers can actually "Manuel" or ride a wheelie all the way through a whoop section, which of course takes great strength, commitment, and skill. Riding whoops at an expert level also requires good suspension, and you will quickly know if you need help in that regard.

Advanced whoops practice:
- Try riding whoops in soft conditions like sand and mud (creating ruts).
- Try staggered whoops and rhythm sections.
- Try bigger manmade whoops on a challenging moto-cross track.
- Try a desert racecourse with big whoops made by trucks with 24-inch or more of wheel travel.
- Try riding desert whoops like those found on the Baja 1000 racecourse that go on for 20 miles or more.

Desert Whoops

1 Desert whoops should be ridden like motocross track whoops, except they are located on both hard and sandy soil that is often strewn with rocks of various sizes.

2 Another unique challenge with desert whoops is they can be much bigger than track whoops, which periodically get groomed by a tractor.

3 Whoops are typically taken in the attack position.

4 Use your arms and legs to help soak up hits and the changing attitude of the bike.

14 Jumping

Jumping is one of the most exciting things you can do on a motorcycle

Jumping is one of the most extreme (as in dangerous) things you can do on a motorcycle, so every jump should be taken seriously. Even on small jumps it's important to attack them and be proactive, otherwise your bike might take over and spit you off. For off-road riders, jumping is practical and fun and can be as mild or wild as you want. To practice jumping you must have correct body positioning and great bike control and you must be focused, confident, and committed. You can start developing your jumping skills safely by using the following step-by-step approach.

How to practice basic jumping

To practice jumping, locate a small jump at first, with a ramp that is smooth and not too steep and has a gentle lip (a takeoff point that is not too steep) and a flat and clear landing zone. Make sure your approach is straight and give yourself plenty of room. Approach the jump in the attack stance, centered over the bike, and be sure to carry your weight on the footpegs, not on your arms. Be prepared to freely move your body fore and aft and even side to side.

When you're taking your first jumps, use a soft, steady acceleration instead of a hard acceleration and hold the attack stance as you climb the jump ramp. As the bike leaves the ramp and you fly through the air, shut off the throttle only after it has left the ramp and pull back on the bars slightly, which will help you land with the rear wheel first. Eventually, it's good to learn how to change your angle in the air to land on either tire first. Never chop the throttle right before takeoff. Doing so will cause the front end to dive and possibly cause an endo.

"Jumping is one of the best parts of riding but it can also be one of the most dangerous. Start small and work your way up. Jumping tabletops are the best type of jumps to gain experience and then you can progress to small, easy double jumps. Be realistic with your skill level. A couple of techniques that are important when jumping are to be standing up and throttle through the takeoff. As you progress you will learn to control the bike in the air by tapping the rear brake to bring the front end down and giving it some gas to bring the front end up."

Jeff Tilton
Supercross and X-Games competitor

As strange as it sounds, the speed of the spinning rear tire can change the angle of the bike while airborne. A quickly spinning rear tire will help bring the front end up, while a slowing or stopped rear wheel helps bring the front end down. That is why at the races you might hear a rider revving his engine wildly while airborne because his front end is dipping too low. You'll also see racers tap the rear brake while in flight to drop the front end either because it's too high (a loop-out) or because they want to land front wheel first on a downslope landing. You can practice these techniques to a small extent once you graduate to the medium and larger jumps.

Uphill jumps are fun (and a little safer) to practice because you don't get very high off the ground. Downhill jumps or ledges can be sketchy if you give it too much throttle, causing you to jump too far or even loop out. Too little throttle off a ledge could cause an endo. When jumping any jump make sure the landing area is clear and there's plenty of room to stop.

Basic Jumps

1 When learning to jump start with a nicely groomed jump like this one on a motocross track that has a smooth and gradual face, making it easier to control the bike in the air.

2 Approach jumps with your weight placed over your foot pegs, leaning your body forward slightly, and be prepared to spring with your legs and jump with the bike as you accelerate all the way up the face of the jump.

3 Too much throttle at this point may make the front wheel go too high during the jump, while chopping the throttle here makes the front end dip. For your first practice jumps try to keep a steady medium throttle and see how that works.

4 Eye your landing area and be prepared to help soak up the impact with your arms and legs.

Once you become proficient at jumping you'll also be able to grip or press against the bike with your legs to help control or stabilize your bike while in flight. Remember, when first learning to jump, start out small and gradually build your confidence and then build your jump height and distance. For more on jumping, see Chapter 21 on motocross jumping.

Natural jumps

Jumps usually found on a racetrack are often manmade, but there are plenty of natural terrain jumps and ledges to practice on at most ride areas. Jumps don't always have to be made of dirt, however. In the right situation you can use a variety of natural terrain obstacles such as rocks and logs off which you can catch air. If you do use one of these natural obstacles for jumping, try to square up 90 degrees to the most favorable surface point of contact and be ready to be kicked up or sideways, as these natural jumping ramps rarely have a good shape for jumping.

Desert Jumps

1 Desert jumps are very unpredictable and could hide a buried rock, gofer hole, or hard dirt kicker that can throw you in a wrong direction very quickly.

2 Again, scout every jump you can very carefully first if you want to ensure success and be aggressive, because one of the most common mistakes in jumping is not going fast enough.

3 This is a good attitude for the bike on a basic, simple jump with the rear wheel just a bit lower than the front.

4 Most riders are surprised to see just how much the bike's suspension compresses, even on a relatively small jump.

Advanced jumping practice:

- Try to land precisely in the same place every time.
- Try a challenging rut-filled jump.
- Try various uphill jumps or ledges.
- Try various downhill jumps and dropoffs.
- Try landing front wheel first consistently off a variety of jumps.

- Try different sized and shaped jumps with a variety of lips or kickers (the lip or kicker of a jump is the last few feet of a jump). Many times a vertical kicker is formed on the lip of a jump from the spinning rear tire. They usually kick the bike higher or more sideways in the air. Kickers must be attacked aggressively or they'll kick you.

Catching More Air

1 Jumps come in a wide variety, so try to always carefully check out the condition of the jump face and the landing zone before you jump.

2 As you fly through the air you can pull back slightly on the handlebars to land rear wheel first, the preferred way to land most jumps.

3 Yep, you're actually flying at this point!

4 Brace for the landing and be ready to absorb the impact with your legs if it's a big jump.

Sitting While Jumping

1 You can jump without standing or using a ramp if you use the classic seat bounce method to bunny hop the rear wheel off the ground.

2 Do this by performing a power wheelie and with good timing quickly spring with your legs and "bounce the seat" and momentarily flick the clutch to raise the RPMs to help increase lift for the jump.

Standing While Jumping

1 Standing up when jumping allows you to use your legs to compress the suspension to prepare for the jump, then use your legs to spring up and...

2 ...help gain altitude and absorb the upcoming landing.

15 Brakeslides and Powerslides

Getting sideways is the key to making quick corners

Brakesliding and powersliding are the quickest and most efficient ways to to tackle many turns on the trail and the race track. Brakesliding is an advanced turning technique where you lock up the rear brake to swing the bike around a corner. There are basically two kinds of brakeslides; one is a long, arcing slide and one is a short, tight angle pivot of 90 degrees or more. Brakeslides are used at turn entrances and are a great technique to use to pass someone in motocross racing or take a tight off-road turn. Brakeslides are a great way to experience sliding a motorcycle for the first time.

How to practice brakeslides

To practice brakeslides, locate a flat, relatively slippery dirt surface with plenty of room. Preferably, practice this where there is a mixture of smooth dirt and fine decomposing sand that provides a consistent feel. Once you've found a good place, position a marker such as a cone or old tire to turn around. At a modest speed approach the left-hand turn entrance in second gear, sitting down and forward (you want the rear wheel to be light). Pull in the clutch, lock up your rear brake, and lean the bike to the left. Do not release the brake until you have stopped. Don't turn the handlebars to the left and lean into the turn until the end of the slide. Keep

"There are many corners, especially late in a race or when the track is beaten down, where it pays to run completely different lines than the other guys. To accomplish that, you have to use a different technique. Whatever it takes to get the bike turned before the other guys is the key, and many times that is to slide the bike into the corner on the rear brake and finish the turn with the throttle so you can get back to full acceleration before the other guys. It's all about lean angle, throttle, and brake control."

Johnny Murphree
AMA National Flat Track Racer, winner of four Nationals, countless podiums, and two series runner-ups

your handlebars straight with the rear brake locked up and lean the bike. How much you turn (or spin out) will be determined by how much you lean the bike and how quickly you lean it. If you lean it a lot and quickly, you will perform a pivot brakeslide turn, which is 90 degrees or more. If you lean it a little and slowly, you will make a long arcing brakeslide. Of course, as you come to a stop, put your left foot out to keep from falling over.

Caution: When learning to brakeslide, keep your speed low and always err on the side of leaning too much rather than not leaning enough. Too much lean will only result in a low-side crash, as opposed to not leaning enough, which might result in a crash to the high side, where you're more likely to incur damage. It's good to practice this and be able to lay the bike down on purpose (crash to the low side) instead of trying to stop upright. Sometimes if you know you're going to crash, it's better to choose the way you will crash, and low siding is actually a safer way to crash.

Advanced brakesliding practice:
- Try to brakeslide to the right; it's more challenging because you must keep the rear brake on while leaning

Basic Brakeslides

1 To practice brakeslides, ride sitting down, pick up a little bit of speed, pull in the clutch, lock up the rear wheel with the brake, and lean the bike.

2 How much you spin around will depend on how much you lean and how quickly you lean the bike.

3 It looks like fun, and it is!

4 When you come to a stop put your foot out or you'll fall right over!

and then put your right foot on the ground at the last minute when you stop.

- Try brakesliding on various surfaces to test traction and lean limits.
- Try brakesliding while riding standing up, to the right and left.
- Try long arcing brakeslides vs. 90-degree pivot slides around obstacles.
- Try to lay your bike down on purpose (as gently as possible).

Powerslides

Powersliding is an advanced turning technique where you can make a turn by spinning the rear wheel while leaning the bike. On the trail, powersliding is usually performed at turn exits and follows an increasing radius arc (instead of the turn getting tighter, it gets wider). Powersliding, or "rear steering," is practical, fun, and very entertaining too. Good powersliding skills are a must if you ever want to give racing a try.

Feet-Up Brakeslides

1 Brakesliding to the right is challenging because you must keep your foot on the rear brake until the last second.

2 Of course, if you practice really hard...

3 ...maybe you can keep your foot on the rear brake....

4 ...all the way through to the end!

When practicing sliding it's always better to err to the side of leaning too much and crash to the low side like this rider is doing, than it is to not lean enough and risk the dreaded high-side crash.

How to practice powerslides

To practice powersliding, locate a flat and fairly slippery dirt surface with plenty of room. Try to find dirt with a composition that provides consistent feel. Position an apex marker (a cone, tire, etc.) and slowly approach the left turn entrance in second gear, sitting down. Make sure to sit forward on the seat and lean forward if needed to ensure the front tire gets most of the grip. As you reach the turn entrance, lean the bike and roll on the throttle quickly to get the rear tire spinning (in many cases on the trail, you can initiate the powerslide with a quick brakeslide turn to break the rear end loose). Try to follow a decreasing radius arc (instead of the turn getting wider, it gets tighter) to force the slide even though you may naturally drift into an increasing radius arc.

Obviously, powersliding is a lot easier when you have plenty of power, but like many developing skills, you will learn more and faster when you first try it on a bike you can really handle that is not too big or powerful. When powersliding on a smaller bike with modest power, you must lean it more and manage its little power carefully. It is better to learn how to master powersliding on a smaller bike with modest power before moving to big power, where powersliding only takes a slight lean and a twist of your right wrist.

Stand-Up Brakeslides

1 For an increased challenge try making stand-up brake slides to the left *and* right.

2 Once you get the brakeslide down, try making a smooth transition from brakesliding the turn entrance to powersliding the turn exit, to the right and left, of course.

Basic Powerslides

1 Practice powersliding by riding sitting down and slowly entering a flat turn in second gear.

2 Next, lean the bike and roll on the throttle.

3 You can control your slide with the throttle and by adjusting your bike's lean angle.

4 Power out and win the race!

There are actually four things going on, all at the same time, that determine how sideways your bike is going to get during a powerslide: body position, amount of throttle, amount of lean, and steering. When you become an expert powerslider, you'll be constantly adjusting all four with subtle moves to make a beautiful, sweeping powerslide that gets you into and out of the corner in the shortest amount of time.

Weight distribution is critical to powersliding. If you have your weight too far back, the bike might want to hook up (grab traction in the rear tire), or you could also lose the front end from having your weight too rearward. With your weight too far forward, you won't lose the front end, but you'll spin too much and stay too sideways. This is where moving your weight slightly forward and rearward can really help the motorcycle to either spin the rear tire and facilitate a turn or hook up and accelerate away. Even if you don't slide forward or rearward, just leaning your torso more or less can really help or hurt the amount of sliding. When practicing powersliding, experiment with moving forward and rearward on the bike and feel what effect it has on increasing or decreasing your powerslide.

Once you're fairly comfortable doing a powerslide, you'll find that more throttle makes you spin out more, and less throttle straightens the bike out. You'll also find yourself countersteering in the middle of powerslide (just like a dirt track sprint car), essentially turning right to go left. Slight changes in the steering, of course, control the amount of sideways you get, too, as well as the amount of lean.

To prevent high siding (crashing by flipping off the bike to the right when you are trying to turn left) while powersliding, make sure you lean the bike plenty, keep the rear wheel spinning, and follow a smooth, slippery line. To prevent low siding (crashing to the left or laying it down to the left while turning left), make sure you don't lean too much, exercise good throttle control, trying to not overly spin the rear tire, and follow a good traction line. Powersliding sounds like it's really complicated, but in most cases, it becomes second nature to many riders after only a few practice sessions.

Powersliding is one of the most fun things you can do on a motorcycle. To learn how to powerslide start with a small bike and gradually work your way up in horsepower. If you can slide a bike with modest power it'll be easy to slide a bike with plentiful power.

If you can powerslide comfortably to the right and left while riding standing up you can really ride over rough terrain quickly, especially in rough, sweeping turns. You can control the traction on your front tire by shifting your weight more forward or rearward.

If sliding the rear tire gets boring, try sliding the front tire at turn entrances, first when sitting, then when standing. For this exercise keep your speed slow, mount up a fresh front tire, and carefully select a place that has a smooth, firm dirt surface with a slight cushion to it.

Practice sliding against objects

A different kind of dirt bike sliding is helpful when you find your front tire and rear tire in completely different lines, such as that found in side-by-side ruts (aka, cross-rutted). To practice this advanced technique, you can try curb sliding or log sliding, which is when you approach a four-inch-high cement curb (or you can use a log, board, rain rut, etc.) at a steep angle in first gear standing up. Place your front tire on the highside and your rear tire on the lowside. As you slowly accelerate, your rear tire will scrub on the side of the short-steep-hard object, allowing you to experience briefly, under controlled conditions, how to ride sideways and use both varied lean angles and throttle control to maintain the slide and steer the bike.

Getting in situations like that is common in dirt riding, oftentimes when you cross-rut, clip a rock, root, or log, or must ride up technical terrain at less than a perpendicular angle. This fun exercise is another great way to practice and become comfortable with sliding in all conditions.

Practice flat tracking

Riding around a flat oval dirt track is one of the best and most entertaining ways to hone your powersliding skills. To practice flat tracking, just set up a small, firm dirt oval with

Powersliding a Ledge

1 Objects like this old telephone pole are great to practice some powersliding (well, it's kinda like powersliding!). Approach it standing up in first gear at a severe angle and wheelie your front tire over it.

2 As soon as the rear tire hits it, be ready to skid sideways and counterbalance with your body.

Powerslides to the Right

1 Powersliding sitting down to the right requires the same technique as turning left, except it is the "weak side" for many right handed people.

2 When sliding to the right, focus on fundamentals like leaning and make sure to practice your weak side turns even more than your strong side turns.

3 We'd like to say that is the reason flattrack racers turn to the left, but it seems to have more to do with that was the direction horses raced around the old dirt tracks.

4 For some extreme off-season practice, try some of this action in the winter on the ice (don't forget a few studs in your tires though).

two (or four for wider turns) apex markers and ride around, gradually increasing your speed until you are racing as fast as you can. You can aggressively attack both the turn entrances and exits, and you can experiment, exaggerate, and even lay it down or crash and gain a better perspective of what is too much and what is not enough. Invite a friend or two to join you, and then you can practice your racing skills like setting someone up to pass, late-braking, block passing, and general racecraft. Flat tracking can be one of the most fun ways to practice and should be a regular part of your dirt bike rider training regimen.

Advanced powersliding practice

- Try powersliding to the right as well as the left.
- Try powersliding at low speeds, then gradually at higher speeds.
- Try powersliding while standing up, right and left.
- Try powersliding on different surfaces—slippery, tacky, etc.
- Try to combo a turn by brakesliding the entrance and powersliding the exit.
- Want to really have some fun? For riders in northern states, put some small ice studs in your tires and go flat tracking on a frozen lake! (Make sure the ice is thick enough, though.)

To practice stand-up powerslides ride in second gear, lean the bike, and roll on the throttle. As you accelerate you can control your slide with the amount of throttle and lean angle you give it. Be sure to position your body slightly forward to keep weight on the front tire for grip and weight off the rear tire so it can spin.

16 Terrain and Conditions

You never know what's around the corner

In this chapter we discuss how to ride a variety of natural-terrain challenges and natural riding conditions that you are likely to encounter while riding off-road. Always remember our three-item checklist of what to think about as you approach a challenging situation: (1) terrain reading is first followed by (2) line selection and then (3) technique execution.

Pavement and concrete

We're mentioning this high-traction surface to make a couple of important points. First, dirt tires aren't made for this surface and slide easily. Dual-sport tires work better, but have their limits too. Second, we've seen people get in just as much trouble from being surprised by sudden high traction as much as sudden loss of traction. Avoid riding on pavement with knobby tires. You will be safer and your tires will last longer because there's nothing that wears out knobby tires faster than riding on pavement.

"Attacking difficult terrain like rocks and logs can be intimidating. Riders need to be confident, smooth, and precise in order to get the job done right. Gripping the bike enough to hold on but staying loose enough to react to the bike moving underneath you is important. Hitting your lines perfectly and being smooth and precise with your throttle control is also key. Stand up, look ahead, and focus."

Geoff Aaron
Ten-time AMA National Trials champion, 73 National Trials event wins, two-time AMA Athlete of the Year, fifteen-time Trials des Nations team manager

Hardpacked dirt

Hardpack is a term used to describe a dirt road or path that has been packed down to a hard, smooth surface. This kind of surface is better for dual-sport tires than dirt tires or knobby tires because the knobs can't dig into hardpack for traction. The problem is hardpack is often found on fast sections of well-traveled dirt roads and is usually covered with a loose surface of dirt, sand, or worse, gravel. These treacherous surfaces are fun to powerslide on but are also an easy place to crash on. But use caution: Because of the high speeds and lack of traction on hardpacked dirt roads, an unexpected decreasing radius turn can be dangerous, especially if there's no shoulder or run-off. Even though a hardpacked dirt surface typically has good traction, it still has limits. Always use caution and keep your speeds in check.

Ruts

Ruts can be created by many things, but most commonly they are the natural result of rain run-off on hillclimbs or across a trail. In the eastern part of the United States, the lower sections of trails can form nasty wheel ruts from dirt bikes that came through during a muddy period. Ruts can be treacherous if you don't handle them correctly. They have been the ruin of many a rider's day.

When you encounter a rut, you usually have to make a quick choice: either avoid it, cross it, drop into it and ride the bottom of it (if it is a rideable rut), or wheelie across it or jump it. If you scrub the inside of a rut while turning, it will try to turn you more. Fundamentally, the problem with riding ruts is people struggle with sticking to a specific line, like our board-ride exercise, which frustrates many students. That ability to stay on a narrow path requires you to be able to comfortably make lean angle changes to the bike while riding

Expect ruts, especially on any off-road downhill routes you may take. There's nothing worse than encountering a downhill rut at speed and not being able to react in time. Be ready to slow down with good front brake skills and change lines quickly by using your good bike leaning skills.

standing up at all speeds in order to steer the bike around ruts or keep your tires in the bottom of a rut. Of course, if you lean the bike at low speed you must shift your hips sideways to counterbalance or you'll fall over. The technique is much like what is needed to steer a bike down a sand wash or to stay on the good line when climbing a hill.

Generally speaking, avoid big, deep rain ruts if you can, but those that cut across your path will eventually have to be crossed or dropped into. To cross a big rut, try to approach it at a perpendicular angle and if you can't ride through it,

Tales from the Trail:
VARIETY IS THE SPICE OF LIFE (AND RIDING TOO)

I grew up in Arizona and rode mostly in the Southwest, where it is usually dry and loose, which is a lot different than the wet and slippery you might find farther east. I discovered this fact brutally when I competed at an AMA Trials National in Missouri where the mud was like ice-covered clay over gorilla snot. This one section was so simple I laughed when I first saw it, but almost cried when I tried to ride it. It was on a slight slope winding around a few trees. There was so little traction I was humbled and happy if I got through each loop with only 3, and not 5, penalty points. After that day, I embrace and practice on especially slippery terrain every chance I get.

you may have to wheelie the front tire across it or jump over it altogether. If you have to drop into a rut that's running parallel to you, be sure to stay in the bottom center and not let your tires scrub the sides. The worst thing is when a rut surprises you like the nasty rain ruts found in Baja on the backside of a rise in the road. For these situations, the best plan is always to reduce your speed and not allow anything to surprise you. Apply the right techniques when you encounter a rut, and it will become just another fun obstacle you can look forward to conquering.

Rocky terrain

Unfortunately, many people fear rocky sections and go around them because they haven't had any experience with rocks and don't know how to ride them. Rock challenges come in a variety of shapes, sizes, and slickness. With the right bike and techniques, most are rideable, some are not. When you encounter rocks, you should use the same old checklist: terrain reading, line selection, and execution. For terrain reading, some rocks have better traction than others. Some are slick because of what they're made of, some are

Big Boulders

1 For larger objects like this rock you can wheelie and roll up it just like a trials rider would do.

2 While in the attack position, pop a quick wheelie at this point.

3 Skim the front tire on top of the rock and...

4 ...get ready to soak up the impact with the rear wheel.

5 Once you know you'll make it over the object, be ready to quickly pull in the clutch and...

6 ...use your brakes to control your speed.

waterworn, or some may be simply too rugged to ride on. Other rocks have plenty of traction because they're weatherworn, made of course materials, or simply laying flat.

Sometimes rocks are solid or firmly planted and will not move, which provides good traction and footing you can count on. Other times they are rollers or smaller (baseball- to basketball-size), loosely packed rocks that move easily (like in rock gardens). Rollers are the most unpredictable and the most difficult kind of rocks for a motorcycle rider to navigate through. With rollers you sometimes just have to try to shift up to lower the rpm, carry some speed, maintain your momentum, and use a soft throttle to help avoid spinning the rear tire too much and deflecting sideways when you hit a roller. In general, read the rocks and apply power carefully and try to get traction only where you can.

Once you have read the rocky section and have picked the traction zones and no-traction zones, you must pick a line over or through the rocks that has the smoothest, most high-traction surface, and of course, once you've selected a line, you must stick to that line by applying the right techniques. That includes moving side to side, shifting your weight forward or rearward to help the front or rear, leaning forward to prevent a wheelie, and accelerating before the rock so you don't have to accelerate on it.

When approaching a rock in the dirt, be careful about spinning your tires in the soft dirt just before the rock and then suddenly hooking up when your rear tire gets to the rock. Look for a dry rock. It will always have much more traction than a rock that is wet or has mud splashed on it by a previous rider (Note: Be one of the first riders). In general, it's a good riding practice to assume the traction's not good and carry some speed.

When riding faster around loose rocks, be careful not to clip a rock, or miss it with the front tire and just clip it with the rear tire. This will cause the rear end to deflect sideways out of control. Also, you should increase your

Rock Gardens

1 Rock gardens contain two kinds of rocks, rocks that move and rocks that don't.

2 The problem is you often don't know which one they are until you're on them.

3 To avoid wheel spin and wheel deflection, try carrying a little speed, but not too much, then short-shift to lower the engine RPMs, cover the clutch, and use a soft throttle.

Deep Sand Turns

1 Riding in deep sand requires that you maintain a brisk pace to keep your tires, especially your front tire, riding on top of the sand instead of digging into it.

2 Since you must ride at speed you'll turn by leaning the bike and turning the handlebars slightly.

3 Get back on the gas as quick as you can after making a turn.

4 Notice how the rider has his weight to the rear to keep the front end as light as possible.

tire pressure considerably when you know you are going to be encountering a lot of rocks on the ride. On a stock off-road bike with stock tires and stock inner tubes, depending on your weight, the speeds, and the terrain you're riding in, you can safely run up to 17 psi for rock rides. At speed, square-edged rocks are notorious for causing flats, so you should always run higher tire pressures or use thicker inner tubes or flat-proof Bib-Mouse tubes (foam-type inner tubes) in slower speed trials tires work well with rocks because they have many super soft knobs that are contacting the rock at any given time. Trials tires are radials that are designed to run at lower air pressures and conform to surfaces better. Riding fast on low-air-pressure trials tires will teach you how to use your legs to absorb or to spring and unload your suspension when riding over square-edged rocks to help reduce the possibility of a flat tire or dented rim.

Also, if you ride in a lot of rocks you'd be smart to install a good skid plate and various other guards to protect vulnerable parts such as the engine cases, radiator, and fork tubes.

Sand

Riding in sand can be one of the most difficult challenges for newbie dirt-bike riders. There's sand everywhere, so if you want to ride off-road you had better learn how to ride in it. Of course, sand is soft and robs power so it helps to have plenty of horsepower. Tires and tire pressures are important for traction in the sand. If there are no hard obstacles for your tires to hit, you can get away with even less than 12 psi.

There are many different types of sand out there. Some sand has larger granules and offers some traction, while other sand is fine or has smaller granules, giving it little traction. Wet sand, however, has a lot of traction and is an absolute blast to ride on.

Riding in sand, first and foremost, requires the right amount of speed to negotiate it properly. If you can see sand coming up, attack it by carrying some speed if you can. If you stop in sand or need to make a tight turn, it is difficult to accelerate back up to speed quickly. Sand riding is a breeze if you maintain the right speed, much like how efficient a boat becomes once it gets up to speed and planes out on water. One of the most important things about sand riding is keeping the front end light by riding more rearward than you normally would. Keep your momentum going by being generous with the throttle, and try not to let the front tire dig in, especially when cornering. When riding in sand it is usually not necessary to maintain a fine line, just relax and "herd the bike"; letting it move a few inches or feet to either side is okay. Riding at speed in a sand wash may give you a nervous feeling as the bike wiggles, hunts, and follows ruts made by previous riders, but don't worry. Just let it wander a bit; however, big rocks are sometimes hidden just below the surface in sand washes. Try not to hit them. Sand washes aren't always smooth or straight, so typically they are ridden standing up.

To practice changing lines at speed while standing up, just like in sand washes or hillclimbs, we use a slalom course on hardpack terrain. See the information on steering while standing up in Chapter 12. Tight turns in deep sand are usually performed while sitting down, much like a motocross flat turn. Use the clutch and throttle to keep the revs up, shift your weight forward, and turn sharply, then quickly shift your weight rearward as you accelerate.

If you go riding in the sand dunes, it helps to use a paddle tire on the rear. Dune riding is a great experience but comes with some unique challenges. First, in most sand dune off-highway vehicle (OHV) recreation areas, whip antennas with flags are required to help riders see each other among the dunes. Another common dune hazard is when the wind erodes the face of a dune and forms a sheer dropoff on the backside of a dune that you may be climbing up from the other side. This is called blow-sand, and a good technique to successfully climb dunes with blow-sand and to avoid others who might be coming up the other side is to turn right or left when you get almost to the top and ride parallel to the dune ridge so you can decide if it's safe to drop down the back side or turn and go back down the face you came up. Dune riding can be tricky. Another common challenge is how hard it can be to see the contours, bumps, and depressions in the sand, especially in bright daylight.

When stopping or slowing down in the sand, use caution because of the tremendous drag that sand has on your wheels. In fact, you can pretty much forget about even using the front brake when riding in sand dunes. The front tire tends to dig in real quick and you could get spit off if the tire gets turned at all. You'll find you'll only need a little rear brake to slow down in deep sand.

Looking for a sand-riding challenge? Try riding slow. Try making tight turns with your inside foot down or with both feet up. Because of the difficulty level of sand there are countless ways to challenge and entertain yourself.

Mud

The techniques used for riding in mud are quite similar to those for riding in sand, except mud is more slippery and dirtier. Basically, the right amount of speed is the most important technique in mud to keep your bike "planed out" like a motorboat when it gets up to speed. The key is to keep accelerating with your weight rearward to keep the front wheel as light as possible, and be ready to move side to side on the bike as it squirms around beneath you.

Of course, there are many different kinds of mud. There's sandy mud, slippery mud, mud that stains your metal, but the worst kind of mud is the sticky, clingy mud with clay in it that clogs your knobs and builds up under your fenders, which

Tales from the Trail:
FORMULA FOR DISASTER

Any combination of riding too fast or while impaired, tired, dehydrated, distracted, in poor visibility, when it's too cold, when it's too hot, and so on are all formulas for disaster that can be avoided if you recognize them and adjust your speed. A common problem for motorcycle riders and racers is that riding can make you extremely tired, which can negatively affect your judgment. Years ago I was racing at high speed in a long Arizona desert race when I encountered a debris island filled with driftwood and cactus in the center of a wide sand wash. Being somewhat "velocitized" due to the speed and fatigue, I was indecisive about going around the island and instead "target-fixated" directly on it, barreling through all the debris like a crash-test dummy! The result was a wild ride and two flat tires, but fortunately no big crash. After that, I vowed I would never be indecisive or target-fixate like that again.

Riding mud takes a certain amount of commitment. Like sand you want your front wheel skimming and your rear wheel grabbing traction so typically you'll have your weight over the rear of the seat.

increases its weight considerably. It's a good idea to stiffen up your suspension if you know you'll be riding in sticky mud.

Half the battle of mud riding is preparing your bike and riding gear for the sloppy stuff ahead of time. First, put fresh tires on that have enough space between the knobs to self-clean. Racers will install foam in voids around the engine to prevent mud from packing up there, and you can glue and wire your handlebar grips to prevent them from loosening up. Your choice of the proper riding gear is important if you want to have a good day riding in the mud. Mud usually means wet conditions as well (see our riding gear preparations for rain and mud in the "Rain and wet" section).

There is such a thing as a mud section being too muddy and too deep for a dirt bike to get through. You have to decide ahead of time if it's actually rideable. If you misjudge and get stuck, you may be there for while. In extremely muddy conditions you can get really stuck and you may actually have to flip your bike over sideways many times to get it out. Riding on muddy days can be miserable if you have the wrong attitude or you're not prepared, but it can also be great fun if you are prepared and embrace the challenge. Just remember it's the same for everybody riding that day, and it is days like these that create some of the best memories.

Rain and wet

Naturally, when it rains you can expect less traction on certain surfaces and you'll have to use some specific riding techniques to compensate. Slippery soil-like clay is downright dangerous for motorcycle riders; however, the right amount of rain on dry sandy soil actually improves traction and creates what we fondly refer to as hero dirt. Generally speaking, rain and wetness can make hard terrain soft and can make soft terrain firmer.

Keep in mind that on an especially rainy day you might cross a stream and just a short time later be unable to return across because the water level has risen too much. In fact, it might not even be raining where you are, but if you're riding down slope from a big storm nearby, you could experience a flashflood. Also, be aware of lightning strikes during thunderstorms, especially in the mountains. Don't take shelter under a tree because lightning strikes trees. Instead, seek shelter in a vehicle, building, or rock outcropping, or some substantial low structure.

The key to successful riding in the rain is preparing your riding gear and bike ahead of time. If you can stay warm and dry, you'll ride better, but if you're too bundled up, you'll overheat, sweat inside, and get soaked anyway. You could don a complete rainsuit and stay completely dry, but you need some movement in your riding gear and some gaps and vents to relieve your body heat.

Enduro jackets specifically made for dirt-bike riders are a great investment and work well in the nastiest conditions. There are a number of ways to prepare your gear for wet conditions: You can put no-fog on your goggles, wear tear-offs on your goggles, seal the tops of your boots with duct tape to keep water out, and carry an extra set of gloves when your first pair becomes too muddy to use.

Be sure to waterproof your bike. You should seal your airbox, waterproof all electrical connections, and route carburetor vents. Make sure your handlebar grips are solidly mounted and even safety wired on because when water creeps in, the hydraulic pressure will eventually loosen the grip and it will start spinning and could come off. The best source for learning the full "race prep" you'll need for these extreme conditions is to look at what the expert riders are doing with bikes like yours.

There's something about riding in inclement weather that's a blast. After a day of feeling cold, wet, and tired, you'll feel good about surviving and conquering conditions that others whine about. In the dry Southwest, we don't get much rain so we try to enjoy and make the most of it when it does

come, especially because it brings with it great traction, cool conditions, and no dust. If you only ride when the weather is fair, you're going to miss out on a whole lot of fun.

Fog

Fog is cold and wet and will dramatically limit your vision. You might ride in fog all day along the coast or it may come and go as you climb and descend hills and mountains. Fog will make you wet, especially along all the leading surfaces of your body and bike. You can prepare for riding in fog by packing a waterproof jacket, pants, and gloves, but one of the biggest challenges in fog is your vision. One of the most difficult conditions is when it is dry and dusty, but the fog rolls in. This results in a thin layer of mud quickly forming on your goggles as you ride. Lens-treatment products like Rain-X will help water run-off and No-Fog will help prevent your goggles from steaming up inside from your body heat. Goggles can be equipped with a Quick Strap so they can be quickly removed and replaced while riding and you can also attach products like lens tear-offs (but please don't litter) or goggle roll-offs that will also help you maintain good vision in challenging conditions like fog.

Water crossings

First, don't attempt a water crossing until you are sure your bike's air intake is sealed and your carburetor vents are routed correctly so they remain open and your bike doesn't stall midstream. It's probably a good idea to test your bike's waterproofing in a local crossing rather than on a long ride.

Most water crossings can be ridden if the water is not too deep or flowing too rapidly (many times this depends on the season). Still water usually is deeper than running water and to check the water's depth you can always use a small tree branch (or throw your buddy in). Remember, in rainy conditions you can sometimes cross a stream and just a short time later not be able to return across because the water level has risen too much.

Select the line that you take for water crossings very carefully. You can expect reduced traction and a slick, often moss-covered rocky bottom. If the bottom is solid rock, you can ride where the water is flowing for the best traction. If it's deep, you must ride slow and steady. It's OK to paddle with your feet in case you hit a big rock hidden in the water. The last thing you want to do during a water crossing is drop your bike. If it's shallow, you can ride a little faster, and you can reduce the splash from the front tire deflecting off your

Relatively deep water crossings with moss-covered rocky beds are really tricky and can humble even the best riders. If you're uncertain check the depth with a tree branch first and also carefully select the best line to take. The main thing is to stay upright and keep moving. Approach standing in first gear and be prepared for your engine to bog, your wheels to spin, and your feet to get wet. Don't worry about "paddling" with your feet if you have to to stay upright.

Crossing slightly deep water at speed like this will result in you and your bike getting a good shower, but maybe you both need one! The problem is water can splash off the front wheel onto your legs and then into the engine/carburetor/air box area, which if not properly water proofed could cause your engine to stall. Note how the rider is dipping his helmet visor to keep his goggles dry.

Crossing slightly deep water can be a relatively dry experience if you simply raise your legs up and ride slowly to avoid the splash. The problem is the bottom could be rough or there could be a hole, so only use this method on your second pass through that section.

legs into your engine area by raising your legs in the air while sitting on the seat.

Some small water crossings or puddles can be crossed fairly cleanly by doing wheelies across them, but use caution and don't underestimate the drag the water will have on the rear tire as you ride through it. That drag could cause the front tire to come down into the water, and the drag from it could cause a violent end-over-end dismount right there in the water if you're really going fast.

Caution: After any water crossing, your brakes won't always work correctly, so lightly apply them as you ride away to dry them out. Also, use caution about crossing water in

sensitive areas and always tread lightly around wetlands. Typically, if the trail comes to a water crossing, that is the best place to cross. Don't make your own new trails across stream and never ride up and down streams for fun. That's a quick way to get the ride area shut down.

If you are unfortunate enough to fall in the water and drown your bike, you're not disabled permanently. The first step to recovery is to drain the airbox, cylinder, and exhaust of water. *Never* try to start an engine that has taken in water without draining it first. Doing so could cause tremendous internal damage. Empty the exhaust system by standing the bike up on the rear wheel with the exhaust tip at the lowest

Tales from the Trail:
SINK-OR-SWIM SNOWMOBILE LESSONS

I could ride a dirt bike really well but had no experience riding snowmobiles when I went to New Mexico to ride them in the mountains with three-time Indianapolis 500 winner Bobby Unser. I was fully expecting to get a lesson or two first, but I was wrong. I guess they wanted to test me. So we took off and immediately started riding off-cambers, tight trails, and steep hillclimbs. Talk about a fish out of water, I couldn't even see the ground I'm used to riding on and got stuck in tree wells and flipped it more than once trying to keep up with Bobby and his brother, Al Sr. (a four-time Indy 500 champ). After two days, I finally figured it out and only had a little time to enjoy it before leaving. I just wish they would have spent a little time teaching me beforehand so I could have enjoyed it more. Just like learning to ride a Jet Ski, a few helpful tips will go a long way. The sink-or-swim method of teaching is a little harsh for most people and in the case of motorsports, more dangerous as well.

point. To empty water from the engine, you should remove the spark plug (always carry a special spark plug wrench) and then with the bike on its side, carefully turn the engine over with the kick start or electric start to pump the water out the spark plug hole. Also, remove the airbox lid and clean all the water out, and you may have to wring out the air filter as well. This can take a while, but chances are you'll be up and running again after performing those steps. It's very important to check your oil as soon as you get home, however. If it's milky, that means water got into the engine case and you should change the oil as quickly as possible. You may even have to do it twice if it was fully immersed.

Snow, ice, and cold

As you can imagine, traction is *very* limited in snow and especially on ice, so you must proceed with extreme caution if you want to stay upright when riding in it. Snow can be ridden on easily with a dirt bike if it's not too deep or too packed down into ice and you can ride on frozen earth, but you can expect it to be hard and lack traction when thawed. If you can, dress in layers so you are able to remove or add clothing as the day (and your body) heats up or cools down. If you're on a real snow ride like those in the northern states, you can take a hint from the snowmobile folks and wear a lot of the same gear that they wear.

If riding in snow at moderate temperatures, prepare to get your feet and hands wet and carry a couple of extra pairs of gloves and dry socks. Some long rides require that we ride through high-elevation mountain passes or ride after dark, so we must be prepared with extra riding gear to pull from our backpack. Pocket heaters are a nice thing to have during rest stops. Serious snow and ice riders in the northern states typically install studs (or small sheet metal screws) in the knobs on their tires to improve traction.

Heat

If you ride in hot weather, always make sure you are well hydrated before and during the ride. You must always carry water with you via plastic bottles or a drink system in your backpack. If you get hot, be careful about drinking too much cold water too quickly when you get back to the ice chest or you can make yourself sick.

Don't forget that many bikes need water too. Water-cooled bikes can boil over radiator fluid if the engine gets too hot, which means you must stop, let it cool, and refill it with water. Also, just because it is hot is no excuse for not wearing all the protective riding gear, because today there are many options of fully vented riding gear. Another trick some riders use in really hot weather is a wet T-shirt or small towel wrapped around their necks. The evaporation really keeps you cool and you can recharge it at every water crossing.

Dust

Dust is one of the biggest pains in the you-know-what when it comes to dirt biking. Dust makes vision and breathing difficult and chokes the engine's air filter. When it's dusty and you can't see well, the obvious thing is to slow down. You can also lay back from the rider in front of you until it clears up and then resume your pace. There's no reason to stay right on someone's tail when it's dusty.

To prep your bike for dusty conditions, make sure you start with a good clean air filter for the day and maybe even be ready to clean that filter overnight or install a new one you previously oiled and carry ready-to-go in a plastic bag. You can also use a great little invention called Filter Skins, which is essentially a sock that covers your air filter that can be pulled off easily once it is dirty, leaving you with a clean filter underneath. To help your breathing in extremely dusty or

Tales from the Trail:
CHOOSE CAREFULLY WHERE YOU RIDE

I once drove for five hours to compete in a trials competition held in a forest with plenty of great riding. After arriving, I quickly unloaded my bike, dressed up, and began to warm up in the designated practice area. Almost immediately when descending a steep hill littered with broken tree branches, one of those branches flipped up into my front wheel and wedged itself into my spokes, breaking about eight of them before I could get stopped. In just minutes I was done for the day, so I loaded up and went home. From that day on I now think twice about riding over broken tree branches and sometimes even carry a spare wheel or two, just in case.

It's no secret that snow makes things pretty slippery. Many riders in the western mountains encounter snow up in the higher elevations. Most would say it makes the ride more fun and challenging!

unhealthy conditions, you can wear a mask to filter out any possible harmful airborne particulates like asbestos.

To prepare your goggles, a good trick is to use a little baby oil on the foam to prevent dust from getting inside your goggles lenses, and you can use dust repellant (Pledge works great) on the outside of the lens. Every time you stop, simply give the lens a quick swipe with the fingertips of your gloves to get the dust off. It's also a good idea to keep a goggles-cleaning kit and two or three spare pairs of goggles prepped and ready to go back at the truck as backups. Finally, most people don't like dust (or dirt bikes) as much as we do, so try not to make too much dust around homes or campsites.

Wind

About the only thing we have to say about riding in very windy conditions is avoid going off of any big jumps. Surprisingly, wind can move you offline to the point of crashing. It's not worth the risk. Riding on a windy day will also dehydrate you and wear you out faster than riding on a calm day.

Elevations

If you're riding in the mountains, the elevation changes in just one day can potentially be thousands of feet, which affects how both you and your engine runs. On a typical MotoVentures multiday guided dual-sport tour in the rugged mountains of the Southwest, we might start riding in the desert at 2,000-foot elevations and within just a few hours climb to an 8,000-foot elevation and ride back down again in a day. A change like that will greatly reduce your breathing efficiency and could even cause altitude sickness (headache, nausea, and more). Temperatures are also greatly affected by elevation, and weather systems (rain) are more likely in the higher elevations, so be sure to take a jacket if you expect to ride in the high country or stay out past sundown.

Most people are quite surprised by how much an elevation change affects the performance of a small engine. The higher you get, the lighter the air becomes, which at a certain point makes your dirt-bike engine run too rich (too much fuel, not enough oxygen). A rich fuel and air mixture makes your engine blubber and produce less power. One thing you can do if you know you are going to be experiencing big changes in altitude during your ride is jet the bike to be slightly lean at the lowest beginning point so it will run better at the highest point. It's a compromise, but it usually works a lot better than if you just left the jetting alone. Of course, if your bike is fuel injected you won't have to worry about jetting for high altitudes.

Logs, ledges, and tree roots

Logs, ledges, and tree roots are the things that really make dirt-bike riding fun. When you encounter a big log or vertical ledge, try to approach it slowly at a 90-degree angle, and just before you get there, do a wheelie and place your front tire on top or into the top part of the obstacle. From there, either skid plate it (let your bike's skid plate slide over it) or perform a roll-up (see trials techniques on page 165) if it's too tall to skid plate it. You can go over logs at less than 90 degrees, but you must be ready for the rear to kick sideways when it deflects off the log. When you're climbing over obstacles like logs and ledges, it helps to unload with your legs, like a bunny hop, to help the rear tire get up and over it too. Tree roots grow in every direction so it's hard to line up on them, and if they are bare or void of bark, they can be slippery. When riding over a slippery log, ledge, or root, it is best to try for traction and acceleration before the obstacle to generate the momentum you need, then shut off the throttle just before the rear tire goes over it.

Dropoffs

If a hill has a place that is really steep, but not too long, you may be able to ride down it by rolling straight down and shifting your weight far rearward to keep from flipping over the bars. If a hill has a place that is too steep to ride down, you may be able to jump off and land front wheel first—if there's enough room. This is why it is good to practice to land on the front wheel by gently floating a wheelie off a small dropoff first, then gradually going bigger as your confidence builds.

Bushes

Bushes (or brush) come in many forms, some with branches that bend and some that are stiff and won't bend. Some bushes have thorns (including all cacti), and some bushes don't. Bushes can snag on your front brake and clutch levers (use hand guards and bark busters). Bushes can also snag on your shift and brake levers (use shift lever and brake pedal guards if you ride in a lot of them). In Arizona, there is a bush we call Cat Claw because it has thorns just like a cat's claw and will rip you to shreds if you try to take a shortcut through it. Generally speaking, always stay on the trail or road and avoid busting through brush because the brush will eventually beat you.

Grass and ground covers

Grass and various ground covers can be treacherous because they are usually wet and slippery. Grass and ground covers can also hide hazards like ruts, rocks, logs, roots, and other bad things you might not be able to see and don't want to run into. If there's grass or ground cover growing, there's water, and maybe too much water. Also, use caution when riding in abundant dry grass or weeds; if some of it rests on your exposed hot exhaust header pipe long enough it could catch on fire. Riding where sensitive plants are growing is a good place to avoid or to practice treading lightly to keep your environmental impact to a minimum.

Crossing Logs

1 If possible, always cross logs at a 90-degree angle.

2 If the log has a modest diameter or an easy approach you can wheelie and place your front tire on top of it and...

3 ...your skid plate will grind over it.

Crossing Big Logs

1 If the log you're crossing has a large diameter or is slightly off the ground like this one...

2 ...you will want to use the roll-up technique where you wheelie into the top part of the object and...

3 ...use it to bounce off and wheelie higher, giving you a little more ground clearance.

Darkness and riding at night

If you know you will be riding at night you can plan for it, but sometimes things happen and you are forced to ride in darkness unplanned to complete your ride. A little preparation can turn a night ride into a fun experience. First, make sure you're riding a bike with reliable lights and some spare bulbs. Things to pack for a night ride include a flashlight (in case your bike dies), clear goggles lenses if you run dark lenses by day, and a jacket, as the temperature will drop considerably after the sun goes down. Riding with just your bike's lights can be tricky, so slow down until you get used to it. There are less peripheral distractions so you can focus only on the lighted path in front of you. One noteworthy hazard of riding at night is that your light will illuminate only the tops and bottoms of ruts, but not the sides, which could cause your tires to slip and send you crashing.

Dark shadows across the road or trail from nearby trees or rocks shielding an early morning or late afternoon sun can hide nasty holes, rocks, and tree roots you do not want to hit. Even in bright sunshine, use caution with shadows and ride through them only when you can see clearly that they are not hiding something.

Fences and mines

When off-road riding, you will likely encounter a fence or two. Always close gates if they were closed when you arrived, and keep an eye out for closed gates that you may have seen open earlier. Mines or excavations are also common in many desert riding areas and can be hazardous if not spotted. Basically, if you come across an area with obvious dirt piles or evidence of mining, slow down, look around, and use caution because there could be an open mine shaft nearby. It doesn't hurt to pile up some rocks or logs around an open hole you may find on a trail to help warn the next fellow dirt biker who happens to come along.

17 Riding Etiquette and Responsibilities

Responsible riders are safer, help keep riding areas open, and leave little impact on the environment

In this chapter, we spotlight the importance of practicing good riding etiquette and always riding responsibly. There are many reasons to ride responsibly, and we hope that anyone who reads this book or graduates from MotoVentures follows them at all times. They'll be considerably safer, better stewards of the environment, and will portray a responsible image to other trail users, ultimately helping to keep riding areas open. Here are some of the golden rules of off-roading:

- **Excessive sound** is the single biggest reason most ride areas are shut down. When riding anywhere except an official racetrack, all off-roaders should do everything they can to keep the sound of their exhaust to a minimum; loud pipes *aren't* cool. There's been a saying in the dirt-bike world for decades that still holds true today: "Less sound equals more ground." In addition, make sure your muffler has a spark arrestor if you're riding in a national forest or anywhere else that requires one.

"When riding off-road, you'll go around countless blind turns. Make sure you look farther ahead and slow down before each turn and stay to the right, that way you can take any line you want in the turn and also avoid someone who might be coming the other way."

Tim Morton
25 year veteran of the Baja 1000, four-time SCORE 250cc Pro Champion, Baja Tour Guide for 15 years

When you're riding or camping in beautiful places like this, leave it as nice as when you came. Off-road riders who litter are one of the primary reasons many great ride areas get shut down.

- *Respectfully share the outdoors* with others who are not there to ride motorcycles. Ride slowly around campgrounds, staging areas, pit areas, and other congested places, and keep your dust and sound to a minimum. When encountering horse riders, livestock, or wild life, if you can see them first, slow way down or stop completely and turn your engine off until they pass to avoid spooking the animals.
- *Practice "treading lightly"* when riding off-road. This means in sensitive areas try not to spin your tires any more than you have to; save that for the motocross track, desert sand washes, and so on. Stay on the trail. In many ride areas it is actually illegal to stray off the designated trails. If you get stuck in soft terrain, don't just sit there with the throttle on and the tire spinning expecting the bike to claw its way out. Get off the bike and push it out while releasing the clutch. Just because you're a good rider and can ride almost anywhere doesn't mean you should ride anywhere you want. Some areas may be sensitive to soil erosion, wildlife concerns, or access and use restrictions. Practice treading lightly and everyone will benefit.

Always stay on designated trails and try to avoid disrupting any wetlands. Don't even think about chasing any critters that may cross the trail!

Some small towns near big trail systems allow off-road riders to ride into town for lunch and a fuel-up. Before a big trip find out ahead of time if that is OK and then make sure you respect that special right by always riding slowly and quietly on the streets.

- **Do not trespass,** respect posted property, and ride only where it's legal and where you're welcome. If you encounter a gate that is closed along an approved route, be sure to close it behind you. Don't expect everything to be posted. You must use good judgment. Generally, the rule on public land is if it is not posted for riding, you probably shouldn't be riding there.
- **Be prepared** for breakdowns, flat tires, and other problems. Carry a cell phone, tools, water, a towrope, and provisions to stay overnight if you have to, and be self-sufficient. Costly rescue missions for lost or injured dirt bikers do not make us look good in the public eye.

- **Always wear your safety gear.** This is not only for your own good, but your riding pals don't want their ride cut short when they have to haul you out injured. It doesn't look good for the local ride area either if the local hospital is getting a high number of emergency room visits from riders.
- **Do not litter.** This is another quick way to lose your favorite riding area and it's easily preventable. Simply follow the rule "pack it in; pack it out." You can even take some extra trash with you. Remember, take only photos and leave only your tire tracks behind.
- **Never ride impaired.** Drinking alcohol or taking drugs and riding is just plain stupid. Riding requires your full

Tales from the Trail:
EXPLORE WISELY

Exploring hidden canyons and remote mountain ranges with your off-road bike is often our quest, but we must be wise and not bite off more than we can chew. I have two personal examples that come to mind. One time my buddy and I rode too far into a rugged remote desert canyon late in the afternoon. It was very technical and we became exhausted trying to get out and ran out of daylight and had no headlights on our bikes. So with one bike stuck, we decided to leave it behind and ride back to camp, two-up and in the dark, and return in the morning with help to get the bike. We definitely could have planned that one better. Another time while we were exploring Death Valley, we underestimated the distance and time that it would take to cross the vast valleys and mountains on the way to our destination. We finally made it back to the hotel, but it was well after dark and we were nearly out of gas—and we supposedly knew what we were doing. It is personal experiences like these that make it easy to see how quickly someone can get in trouble while exploring with your dirt bike if something unexpected happens.

attention and is dangerous enough as it is. Why handicap yourself and increase the risk? Besides, aren't you having enough fun as it is?

• **Don't chase the animals.** I don't feel we need to expound on this.

• **Represent.** Remember, to all nonriders, you represent all riders. Please, represent us well.

How to ride in a group

One of the first rules of off-road riding is never to ride alone; always use the buddy system. Find a good riding buddy or two or three and start with and stay with each other until the ride is over. You should designate a leader and a sweep rider. No one should ever pass the leader and the sweep should never pass anyone. Also, tell someone back home where you're going and when you expect to return.

On a trail ride, each rider is responsible for the rider behind him or her. Stop at all intersections and make sure the following rider sees which way you're going. This is very important to keep anyone from getting lost. If you see a dangerous obstacle ahead or a challenging section, caution the rider behind you with a raised hand.

At the minimum, you should always carry a cell phone, and new technology allows us other communications tools to carry, such as satellite phones and the new Spot Locator device that follows and pinpoints your location by satellite and allows others to track you and know you're okay. It's also a good idea to let everyone know you're leaving your truck keys in a secret place near the truck. That way, if you can't return to it, someone else can get it for you.

When riding with others, don't follow too closely or you may get roosted by the person ahead of you. If you want to ride close, don't ride directly behind someone. Position yourself a little off-set from them so you won't run into them if they stop and you will be able to see around them to spot hazards as well as avoid their dust or their roost. When following, you must decide to either ride close enough so the dust doesn't affect you or you must drop back a good distance so the dust is able to dissipate by the time you get there. When following and the rider ahead must negotiate a challenging hill or river crossing, drop back or stop and watch and make sure the other rider will make it. By laying back, you can learn from other riders' mistakes and also avoid getting caught up in it. If you're riding in front, be kind and try to control your bike's roost so you don't spray others behind you or those you're passing. As a general rule of thumb, always ride for the person behind you.

While riding in a group you are responsible for making sure that the rider behind you makes the correct turn when approaching any Y- or T-intersections.

There are a few common hand signals that are often used when riding with others. Of course, you can use street-rider hand signals to indicate that you are stopping or turning right or left. When you encounter others traveling the opposite direction, you can also hold up your hand with the number of fingers to indicate how many riders are following in your group so they can expect and avoid them. If there's nobody following you, it is helpful to hold up a closed fist to indicate there are no more riders in your group.

If you want to pass someone, be patient and make sure you do it in a safe place with plenty of room. Most people will pull over when they know you're coming up behind them. Be careful not to surprise someone you want to pass and only yell or rev your engine as a last resort to get the other rider's attention. Always be careful with the roost from your rear tire and wait to gas it hard until you are clear of the rider you are passing. Remember, motorcycles are usually the fastest moving vehicles off-road, so if you ride one expect to encounter slower traffic and learn how to pass safely and politely.

Before every ride, tell everyone in the group where you're going and roughly how long it will take. Orient

Many ride areas have sound restrictions. Find out ahead of time what the limits are and make sure you are legal so you don't waste a trip. Most well-maintained stock exhaust systems will easily pass the sound checks.

Even though dirt biking is kind of a "wild" sport, there are still rules and regulations on many trail systems. Follow them or risk getting a ticket.

everyone in the group to your intended directions and note how the sweep of the sun throughout the day relates to those directions. Point out distinctive landmarks if you can. If you do get lost or separated from your group, don't panic. Stop and stay on the trail and make a plan; don't make the situation worse by overreacting. You can periodically shut off your engine and listen, and you can run your engine to let others hear you. If you have to, go to higher ground so you can see others or a road out of there. Ultimately, you must decide if you're better off letting someone find you or if you must find your own way out. Start by backtracking, but be careful not to run head-on into your buddies who may be trying to find you.

18 Bike Preparation

The key to a great ride starts in the garage

Although an entire book could be written about maintaining and modifying your dirt bike, in this chapter we'll attempt to at least fill you in on the basics of what you'll need to know as far as setting up your bike for your specific riding style and terrain. All bikes come from the manufacturer designed and set up for the average-size rider who has an average amount of riding skills. The bike would also be set up to work well, but not great, in just about every type of terrain found in the country. But of course, as we all know, few of us are exactly average in all those areas. That's why we have to set up our bikes the best we can for our size, skill set, and the typical riding conditions found in our area.

First, set up your bike for you

The first thing you can do is personalize your bike's adjustable ergonomics (how something fits you) to fit your body and personal preferences. It's kind of like how you adjust the seat and

"Treat your bike as if you are a cowboy and the bike is your horse. If your bike was a horse you wouldn't just throw a leg over it and go, you would always make sure she was fed, watered, shoed, etc., before heading out on a ride. Be sure to prep your bike at the proper intervals by cleaning the air filter, changing the oil, servicing the chain, bleeding the brakes, adjusting the cables and controls, lubing all pivot points, checking tire pressures, and a general 'nut & bolt' check. After a ride, clean and survey your bike as soon as you can so you have a head start on replacement parts you may need or work you need to do before the next ride. If you wait to prep your bike at the last minute on Friday night it could literally 'throw a wrench' into your Saturday morning riding plans."

Dave Pyle
Nine Consecutive Baja 1000 Overall Wins, National Hare and Hound Champion, Kawasaki Team Green Field Technician and Race Mechanic

steering wheel in your car. With a motorcycle, the seat, handlebars, pedals, and levers are adjustable. After a short time of riding, you'll get a feel for what positions you like. Be sure to keep in mind, however, that with a dirt bike your controls should be comfortable to operate while both sitting and standing.

You can tell a lot about a rider's style by the way a rider has his or her bike set up. For example, when riders have their handlebars slanted rearward, it indicates they prefer to ride sitting down. When their bars are more upright, it indicates they ride standing up a lot, which is also true when they keep a high rear brake pedal height. Your shift lever is mounted on a splined-shaft so it can be raised or lowered a few degrees in each direction. Keep in mind it moves on a sweeping motion, so if it is raised too much, your foot motion to shift up will need to be both upward and rearward. Position your clutch levers so you don't have to strain to reach them when leaning rearward when riding down a steep hill or when leaning forward to climb a steep hill. Adjust the free play out of the throttle, but make sure it still fully returns closed when turned full-lock both ways. Your front brake and clutch levers need a little bit of free play and can be adjusted to engage early or later in their stroke.

A great tip that can save you many broken or bent levers is to wrap Teflon plumbers tape around the bars where the clutch and front brake perches attach to allow them to spin instead or break or bend when you crash.

And when stock doesn't cut it anymore, you can purchase new controls such as footpegs, handlebars, pedals, and levers that are lighter, stronger, better fitting, better looking, and sometimes even guaranteed unbreakable. If you are taller or shorter than average you can install higher or lower handlebars or a higher seat. Really short riders can install lowered seats and also suspension-lowering kits that will make the seat height lower, but will cost some suspension travel.

Replacement handlebars come in all shapes and sizes and they come wide so that they can be cut down to fit smaller riders. Woods riders and racers must cut their bars down to 30 inches and install hand guards to help them ride (fit) through the densely packed forests. A good way to position your bars is to mount them loosely, then sit on the bike in the correct position (center or forward with torso leaning slightly forward). Then close your eyes and reach out where you think the bars should be, then position and tighten the clamps. They should be relatively comfortable in either the sitting or standing riding position.

There is an endless list of valuable accessories you can buy for your bike to protect it or improve its performance. Here are a few we recommend: guards to protect components such as skid plates, disc brake guards, radiator braces, hand guards, and unbreakable clutch and front brake levers. You also have many different types of tires to choose from, ranging from those designed for soft, medium, or hard terrain, and you can install heavy-duty flat-resistant inner tubes if you do a lot of riding in rocks.

Finally, you can improve the creature comfort of your bike by installing rubber-damped handlebars, more

Wash your bike after each ride, lube it up, start it up, and put it away ready to go again. Be careful not to use too much pressure and force water and grit into tight places, and finish up by spraying all those tight places and bare-metal surfaces (*not* your brakes) with a water-dispersant like WD-40.

If you ride off-road you will eventually have to fix a flat and need to mount up a fresh tire someday. Tricks to make it easier include setting your tire in the sun to soften it beforehand. Also be sure to break the bead on both sides, and use some good long tire irons.

For long rides take time to pack your bags carefully beforehand. With tool bags, inner tube bags, front number plate bags and saddlebags, and some creative packing, you can carry much of the weight on your bike and not on your body.

comfortable grips, and even footpegs that will reduce vibrations and increase your comfort. On some bikes you can install a larger fuel tank for greater range, and cold-weather off-road riders can even install heated grips and seats.

Second, set up, service, or upgrade your bike's suspension

Generally speaking, recreational off-road bikes come with softer suspension springs than those found on motocross bikes that need stiffer springs to handle the big jumps. Your suspension is one of the easiest, quickest, least expensive, and most beneficial adjustments you can make on any motorcycle to customize it for you and maximize its performance.

You can easily adjust your bike's suspension by yourself to suit your weight and riding skill level. First, open and read your bike's owner's manual about how to set up your suspension. When you press your hands down on the seat in the middle of the bike, does the suspension move up and down together or does one end move more than the other? It should move up and down freely and evenly at both ends. Next, sit on the bike wearing all your gear and set the suspension sag (as described in the owner's manual). Next, place the compression damping and rebound damping settings in the middle positions (for example, if your shock has 16 rebound damping positions, put it on number 8) on both the front forks and the rear shock. Your goal will be a bike that is balanced in front and rear, with both set up to be

firm or soft, depending on your preference. If one end is off, it will negatively affect the bike's overall handling.

Next, take a fast ride on a trail or section of track that you know well. Try to feel what the bike is doing. Is it bottoming out? Are the wheels rebounding too quickly and kicking you sideways? After testing the bike, adjust your suspension to almost fully firm or fully soft settings. Go for another ride and feel the difference, then change it again in the other direction and go for another test ride. Feel the difference? Do you like the standard settings? Do you like it better soft or hard? If you end up with the settings full hard or full soft you may be ready for some aftermarket springs and valve changes. On most stock suspensions you can only expect to get about a 30 percent change (of the overall range) from full soft to full hard, more if it has been modified. Make sure you're using the full travel of your suspension so that it occasionally bottoms out on the biggest bumps or jumps you ride on. Keep in mind if the conditions are muddy your bike will gain weight and handle differently. Generally speaking, for soft terrain conditions like sand and mud, use firmer settings, and for firm or hard terrain, use softer settings.

If you have a used stock bike, you might find that your suspension only needs servicing, where the oil, seals, and bushings are replaced to give it new life. If that doesn't do enough then you might consider going with aftermarket suspension modifications like Race Tech offers. You can do it yourself and purchase their springs and other equipment, or you can take off and send in your front forks and rear shock and they'll do it for you. Tell them what bike you ride, your weight with full gear on, and your skill level: novice, intermediate, advanced, or pro. Also tell them where you ride and how you like to ride. They will give you the spring and damping modifications you need and all you have to do is install, set your sag, then test ride and dial in your rebound and compression settings.

Third, set up and adjust your bike's engine

Before you make any changes to tune your engine, first read your service manual. It is filled with all the information you need to tune your stock bike. But if stock isn't good enough there is a wide range of engine modifications that includes changing the displacement (increase the size of piston and bore), increasing compression, changing the ignition, changing the carburetor or fuel injection map, and changing the exhaust pipe and muffler. After all, your engine is simply a reciprocating pump with intake, compression, ignition, and exhaust adjustments and plenty of performance-enhancing options.

Even new bikes can use some tuning to their carburetor jetting and suspension settings, which will continue to change as the bike ages and wears. If new, ask the dealer what the hot set-up is for jetting. Many bikes come very lean (minimum fuel-to-air ratio) to meet strict emissions standards and must be richened by installing new carburetor fuel jets. As a rule of thumb, if you climb in altitude, you'll have to lean out your main jet one size for every 2,000 feet past 6,000 to compensate for the thinner atmosphere and reduced compression.

Does your bike idle and run smoothly? This is especially important on small beginner bikes with operators who need to concentrate on learning how to ride. If your bike won't idle, the small pilot jet could be clogged from sitting too long. Small bikes often have this problem because of the tiny jets in their little carburetors. The only way to properly fix this is to clean your carburetor (see your owner's manual).

Safe Loading Procedure

1 It can be tricky loading a bike into the back of a pick-up truck, the most popular dirt bike transporter on the planet. Here is one good way that works even if you're short; first, strategically place a step to help you climb up into the truck bed.

2 Push hard and pick up enough speed to get the front tire up the ramp and into the truck bed, then stop with the front brake holding you in place.

3 Next, climb up on the step and use your left hand to rotate the rear tire forward a little to get the rear tire into the bed and...

4 ...then step up and finish pushing the bike forward into the bed.

If you ride off-road you'll eventually need to perform maintenance and repairs and having a good workshop like this makes it a lot easier. Essentials include good lighting, a heater and a cooler, a refrigerator, plenty of tools, lots of bench space, a vice, plenty of lubes and chemicals, an air compressor, and a bike bench like this one so you don't have to bend over to work on your bike.

If your bike doesn't run smoothly at low rpm on some bikes you may need a special screwdriver to adjust the fuel screw on your carburetor (on a two-stroke, adjust the air screw; it is located behind the slide on the side of the carburetor). A good place to start is 1.5 turns out for either screw. Warm up your bike and adjust the idle (thumb) screw until it idles. Next, start turning the fuel or air screw out a quarter turn at a time until the rpm is at its highest, then adjust the idle back down to normal.

Jetting changes will soon be a thing of the past with the ever-increasing popularity of fuel-injected bikes that automatically adjust to air and altitude changes. The best part is they are fully and quickly adjustable by simply plugging your bike to your computer and changing the bike's fuel and ignition maps for more (or less) performance.

You can also tune your bike's gearing to suit your preferences or the conditions you ride in like high-speed deserts or low-speed woods. You can change your front and rear sprocket sizes, which will slightly lengthen or shorten your chain length and wheelbase. The rule of thumb is changing one tooth in the front sprocket is worth changing approximately three teeth on the rear sprocket. It is better to keep the front sprocket large to reduce

chain wear and the rear small to reduce exposure to rock damage. Dual-sport and recreational bikes usually have wide-ratio transmissions, allowing them to achieve higher top speeds than motocross bikes, which only need to be geared for the longest straightaway.

One of the first things people often change on their engine is the exhaust pipe and muffler. Doing so can increase performance but can also decrease performance if the engine is not tuned for that particular pipe or muffler. Nearly every aftermarket pipe comes with recommended jetting changes to get the full performance out of it. Most aftermarket exhaust pipe suppliers offer options for both their pipes and their mufflers that are tuned for your preference: improved low rpm, midrange, or high-rpm power. If used for off-road and dual-sport, make sure it has a spark arrestor inside. Racing exhaust pipes are very loud and sold for racing only and shouldn't be used for off-road or dual-sport riding.

If your bike is computer-controlled and directly or fuel injected and you replace the pipe, you will need to download new settings or maps to your bike's computer that control everything instead of manually adjusting your jetting. Computer-controlled bikes automatically adjust for altitude and temperature changes and are easily adjustable once you learn how.

Finally, if you still want more power you may be able to increase your engine's size. If you are mechanically inclined, you can purchase and install an aftermarket hop-up kit yourself, which could include a larger piston and bore, new pipe, and a carburetor. You can also take your entire bike or just your engine to a qualified mechanic who can do it all for you.

Here are a few more popular modifications available today for your off-road bike:

- Automatic clutches can virtually eliminate stalling the engine in challenging terrain and eliminate the need to use the clutch all the time (though you can if you need to).
- Steering dampers can be installed to help slow down the oscillating movement of your handlebars that can occur when riding rough terrain at high speed.
- Trials tires can be installed on off-road bikes for improved traction when riding on rocks.
- Foam tire inserts (tubes or balls) can be installed to eliminate flat tires.

19 From Dirt to Street

The top 10 reasons why dirt-bike riding is great for street-bike riders

Almost everyone agrees that many of the skills learned as a dirt rider transfer directly into street-bike riding. It can be argued that street-bike riders with a strong dirt-riding background have much better bike control, more awareness, and are safer riders overall than those who have only ridden in the street. So, with no apologies to David Letterman, here is our Top 10 list of why dirt-bike riding is great for street-bike riders:

1. Dirt bikes are a better tool for the job of learning how to ride.

Dirt bikes are smaller, lighter, easier to control, and more confidence-inspiring. If you want to become a better rider you must practice on a small bike that you can easily control and doesn't have any physical limitations. Street bikes are heavy and hard to control at low speeds. Dirt bikes are also very responsive and provide immediate feedback, so you will learn more and quicker in the dirt than anywhere else. Riding dirt bikes will speed up the learning process. You will learn more in a few months of dirt riding than you would in years of street riding. Dirt riding is also harder and more demanding than street riding. If you can ride a dirt bike well, you can ride a street bike, but not

"Riding off-road and dirt competition was one of the hallmarks of so many of America's top road racers over the past five decades; it's hard to ignore its benefits. This is also true for street riders. Education is irreplaceable because saddle time doesn't always guarantee competence, but a combination of the two is unbeatable. Learning how to handle dirt is a well-scaled ramp up to most any kind of riding."

Keith Code
Founder and director of California Superbike School, author of A Twist of the Wrist

necessarily vice versa. In a perfect world, everyone would start on a dirt bike. Dirt bikes are simply a better tool for the job of learning how to ride a motorcycle correctly.

2. Dirt bikes are better to develop your "feel" for motorcycle controls.

The feel we're talking about here is the fine, delicate feedback you get through your butt and your feet and hands on the controls (clutch, throttle, front brake, shift lever, and brake pedal), along with the simultaneous application of those various controls. On the dirt, you can feel more easily for threshold braking, lean angles, the friction zone of the clutch, sliding tires, and precise shifting and throttle control. Good feel comes when all your senses and muscles are working together. Dirt biking helps you "become one" with any motorcycle you ride.

3. Dirt is a better place to learn braking and turning skills and their limits.

Braking and turning are two of the most important fundamental skills you must have to ride a motorcycle properly and natural *terra firma* is the best place to learn and develop those skills. To be good at serious braking you must practice by exceeding the limits consistently and safely to develop a feel for operating right at the limit, where braking is best. For obvious reasons, dirt is the best place to reach those limits. In the same way to be good at serious leaning you must

practice by leaning too much and low siding to better understand the limits. With proper leaning skills learned in the dirt there's a greater chance you'll be comfortable when the tires do slide on pavement so you don't panic and overreact.

4. Dirt is a better place to become accustomed to speed.

Dirt bikes are fast, but they're slow compared to the acceleration and sheer speed that a street bike can attain. Not many people are prepared and qualified for how fast street bikes really are. The truth is, most people will only go as fast as they feel comfortable with, regardless of their engine size. Why not learn to walk before you run? Concentrate on control in the dirt first where speeds are slower. Improve your control, which builds your confidence and eventually you'll be going faster both on the dirt and in the street.

5. Dirt bikes are designed for crashing so you can better explore the limits.

You won't want to try new techniques and explore your limits if you're worried about crashing and hurting your bike or yourself. Fortunately, dirt bikes are small and light and they are built to endure many crashes and loamy dirt is much softer than asphalt. To ride a dirt bike well you must not be afraid to crash in order to have a true perspective of what its limits are. This knowledge will help you in the street, where you won't have to crash to learn the same lessons.

Dual-sport riders get the best of both worlds. Because they can ride on the street, they can really put the miles in on any given day.

Most motorcycle experts agree that a strong dirt riding background is one of the best, and safest, ways to become a top-notch street rider.

6. Dirt riding develops improved visual habits.

Reading the terrain is one of the most important fundamentals of dirt-bike riding. The countless surface and angle changes in the terrain force you to pay close attention to all the details that lie ahead. If you want to ride motorcycles of any kind, you must become proficient at reading the terrain correctly and always scanning for hazards. In the dirt those hazards may be sand, rocks, mud, ruts, dropoffs, and so on, while in the street the hazards could be sand, water, spilled oil, potholes, railroad tracks, cars, construction, pedestrians, pets, and more. Better to first become an expert at scanning ahead in the dirt than to deal with more serious problems in the street.

7. Dirt is a better place to learn good riding judgment.

Riding any motorcycle requires excellent judgment, a healthy respect, good timing, and the ability to respond correctly. It is better to develop good judgment at lower speeds in a more forgiving environment like the dirt than on the street where misjudging something will have more dire consequences. Good judgment includes choosing when to go or stop, taking this line or that line, or to follow your buddy—or not. We can't teach someone good riding judgment, but it can be learned safely and developed by riding in the dirt first.

8. Dirt riding is a better place to learn how to help your bike.

In the dirt you learn how to lean, move forward and rearward on the seat, stand up, and move your body from side to side, all in an effort to help your bike do what you want it to. You can't move much on a street bike, but it doesn't take much body movement to help it a lot. In the dirt there's no such thing as moving too much and you quickly learn how your body position can really help (or hurt) your bike's handling. By the time you hop on a street bike, you'll already have a great knowledge of weight transfer, and it should be a snap.

9. Dirt riding is a better place to learn the importance of staying on line.

Since your only contact patch on a motorcycle is two skinny, little tires, not sticking to your preferred line can cause big problems. It's a no-brainer that it's better to learn this in the dirt at moderate speeds than it is on the street at higher speeds. A good example is if you happen to completely miss your preferred line. If you blow it in the dirt you may simply run wide on the trail and ride off into the bushes, but if you don't take the correct line on the street you could hit something on the road like gravel, potholes, and curbs and crash. Or you could run wide in a corner and hit something really solid, like a parked car or telephone pole.

10. Dirt is a better overall environment for learning to ride motorcycles.

Besides the fact that a dirt surface is much more forgiving than pavement, there are also far fewer distractions out on the trail than on the street. There are no cars or pedestrians to avoid, traffic laws to obey, or pretty girls walking along the sidewalk to distract you. Sure, there are hazards in the dirt, but they're nothing like the abundant distractions found on the street. Dirt riding is where you should learn to become a great rider so that when you hit the street, those skills will better ensure that you never make a big mistake in that less forgiving environment.

20 Motocross

The most extreme sport on the planet

Motocross racing is easily the most intense form of off-road motorcycle racing. In this chapter, we'll cover the essential techniques required to ride and race on a motocross track. Typically off-road riders will have a couple of years of trail riding under their belts before they attempt to enter any sort of race. A motocross track *is not* a good place for beginners to learn to ride. Many riding techniques needed for motocross are quite similar to what we have already learned in the earlier chapters in this book and out on the trail.

As with any type of racing, speed is the name of the game. Your goal is to ride all the challenging obstacles around the track as quickly as possible. Racing motocross competitively requires specialized skills, tremendous physical fitness, determination, and the bravery to ride fast, catch big air, take chances, and push the limits. Motocross is one of the most physically demanding sports in the world, and even the most fit riders are usually pretty whipped at the end of a long moto. The stadium version of motocross is supercross, which is typically more challenging with shorter approaches to big jumps and tricky rhythm sections.

If you are just getting started in motocross, don't start on a supercross track. You're best to start out on a decent outdoor motocross track, preferably one that has been prepared and watered. Try to take your first laps when the track isn't too crowded and try to choose one that has modest jumps with easy landing areas so you can gradually build your speed and gain your

"You have to be fully dedicated to your physical conditioning to race motocross. You don't have to be the best rider, but if you're in the best condition, you can still win."

Gary Jones

Four-time AMA National Motocross champion, America's first national motocross champion (1971), Baja 500 winner, owner/operator Gary Jones Motocross School

"Ultimately, most riders think that the way to go faster is to have more courage. The truth is, going faster is a matter of technique."

Paul Thede

Owner of Race Tech Suspension

confidence. Of course, to properly practice motocross you'll need a motocross bike, the newer the better because they evolve so quickly. Off-road bikes can be used for motocross, but they're heavier, have less power and softer suspension, and basically, are the wrong tool for the job.

It's important to take the time to prepare yourself and your bike for what you will face on a challenging motocross or supercross track. Start by mastering all the basic trail-riding skills in this book and the specialized skills in this chapter and then you'll be ready for more advanced motocross training and coaching.

How to practice motocross starts

The start of any race is your best chance to pass as many riders as possible at one time. It's always best to pass your competition as soon as possible, otherwise it becomes more difficult as the race goes on. The time spent practicing starts will give you the advantage you may be looking for and will keep your reaction times sharp. How important is a good start? Let's face it, if you're fast enough to ride in front, why not start in front?

To practice starts, locate an appropriate straightaway, preferably an actual motocross starting line. You can use an official starting gate, or just have a friend drop a hand. When using a starting gate, place your bike approximately 12 inches behind the gate and instruct your gate operator to drop it at different intervals to try and surprise you. When you're at the races, carefully watch the starting procedure for the races before you and look for the best line or starting spot if you get a choice.

When the 30-second signal is given, position your body with one or two fingers on the clutch lever, one finger on the front brake, and both feet on the ground. Sit toward the front of the seat, with your upper body leaning forward and your head directly above the handlebars. Rev the engine so that the throttle is about a quarter open, and hold the clutch at the engagement point. Once the gate drops, let out the clutch and twist the throttle. Gradually release the clutch completely and manage the friction zone. Make sure not to spin the back wheel too much, or you will lose acceleration. The whole idea at the start is to make that perfect launch with minimum wheelspin, maximum traction, and a front wheel that doesn't shoot skyward.

Starting lines at most major tracks today use cement pads that provide consistent performance for all competitors. If you race with cement pad starting lines, practice them whenever you can so you can get used to their feel, which is quite different than dirt. When starting on a concrete pad you'll need less throttle and more weight over the center of the bike. Hardcore racers will sweep any dirt off the cement pad and may even do a burnout to help warm up the tire for an improved hook-up. As you progressively release the clutch and the bike accelerates, slide rearward on the seat to help the rear tire hook up and gain traction in the dirt.

Every bike has a different clutch-engagement point that can be altered to suit a rider's preference. If riding a bike with abundant horsepower, you can start in second or even third gear. Motocross bike clutches take some abuse at the start and on the track in every race, so make sure you maintain and service your clutch regularly to ensure the best clutch performance. Most people start with both feet down until they're well off the start, then they pick them up and begin shifting up or speed shifting, which involves slightly "fanning" the clutch for each shift while keeping the throttle on. Of course, shorter people will need to start with only one foot on the ground. Be careful not to pick your feet up too quickly. You need to keep the bike pointed straight and get the power down for the critical first few feet. As you accelerate down the start straightaway, you'll need to keep your bike pointed straight and maybe in a wheel track or rut that runs down the straight. For that, move your body off the sides of the bike and lean the bike to steer it.

Any drag racer will tell you the race is often won or lost on your reaction times and how well you can accelerate in

Practice and perfect your motocross starts on both dirt and concrete starting lines and utilize a backward dropping starting gate whenever you can. When it comes to practicing starts, the more people you can race against, the better. For concrete starts you can use less RPM and sit back a little for added traction. Starts are certainly worth practicing—if you're fast enough to run up front, why start in the back?

Turns usually have an outside line that can be used to "rail" around and carry your speed. For this type of turn enter it a little too fast and plan to use the berm to help slow you down. Once you are locked into the line, accelerate hard all the way around for a high turn exit speed.

the first 60 feet or so. Visualize it before you start, concentrate on the gate movement, and react quickly with the right actions and you'll have a chance at taking the holeshot (the term used for winning the start of an MX race). Starts are the most crowded and possibly most dangerous part of a race—all the more reason to get a good start and get your handlebars ahead of the competitors next to you as soon as possible.

How to practice motocross turns

There are many types of turns in motocross, and track designers purposely build a variety of turns for you to deal with on any given track. During the event, those turns take on different shapes and change considerably with wear as the day goes on. In practice before the race, you can have the fast line figured out, but if you don't adapt to the best lines as the course changes you may get passed by someone who does. Often more can be lost by making mistakes in a turn than can be gained by going faster. The real trick is to hit your lines, concentrate on the fundamentals, and try to get a good drive out of the turn to carry more speed down the next straightaway.

Generally speaking, it is usually best to take, and protect, the inside line. It's the shortest line, but may not set you up or allow you to gain enough speed for a jump placed after the turn exit. You end up with about four ways, or combinations of ways, for making every turn: (1) you can take the tight inside line, (2) you can use a powerslide to help rotate the bike around the outside, (3) you can use a berm to bounce or square off a turn (make a tight pivot and change directions quickly), or (4) you can rail (ride as if on a rail, as on a railroad track) around the turn at high speed against a berm or in a rut. Bottom line: Concentrate on developing good turning fundamentals and avoid making mistakes in the turns to get an advantage over your competition and the quickest lap times.

Bermed turns are turns with dirt built up on the outside of the turn, either by a tractor or by the bike's tires sliding and slinging dirt to build up and create a natural berm. Berms help riders bounce off a rail to change directions. Bermed turns are found on all motocross tracks. Good use of berms or having the ability to square off or diamond a turn will allow you to make fast turns and block pass your opponents or set them up for an inside pass in the next turn.

To practice bermed turns, try to locate one with moist and slightly loose soil like you would find on a prepared motocross track. As you approach, you will be standing up in the attack stance until the last minute when you brake, downshift into a lower gear, sit down and slide forward on the seat, lean the bike aggressively, and stick your inside leg out and forward for balance, to slide on the ground, or to be ready to put your foot down if needed to keep from crashing. You should practice approaching a bermed turn from both the ideal angle and less than ideal angle and make both right- and left-hand turns, just as in a race. With bermed turns your entrance speed can be higher and you can use less brake power because you can use the berm to help slow you down and change your direction. Make sure you're in a gear that will allow you to accelerate. As you hit the berm, you can "fan the clutch" slightly (with two fingers) to raise the engine rpm so you can spin your rear tire to help you rotate and to give you enough power to blast away from the turn.

Flat, high-speed sweeping turns require a completely different approach. You can powerslide the exit to help rotate the bike, or with the right soil, you can rail around a turn and carry a high exit speed by using existing or creating your own smooth, constant-radius berms. Railing

a bermed or rutted turn can be accomplished standing or sitting, depending on how bumpy it is and how well you can ride.

Sometimes it's easier to just remain standing in sweepers because the high speed creates acceleration bumps or whoop-de-dos for you to contend with in the sweeper. Always look for the fastest line, which might not always be the smoothest line. Try to avoid braking and acceleration bumps if you can. Never coast in a turn, use good brake control in the entrance, and get back on the throttle quickly and smoothly on the exits. Always look for the fastest lines and be willing to switch lines if you think it is better or needed to pass. Ultimately, whenever changing directions in a turn, always try to maintain your speed no matter what line you choose.

How to practice motocross ruts

Ruts are very common in motocross, especially where the soil or sand is soft. Ruts can be found almost everywhere on a track: in the corners, on the straights, through the whoops, and on the jump faces. The key to riding ruts is staying out of them or staying in them. That means having the ability to move your body from side to side to keep the bike on

Changing Lines

1 You can change lines by squaring off a bermed turn and turn early, maybe to set up someone for a pass or to simply stay out of someone's roost.

2 Avoid locking into the same line every time; they will change throughout the race.

the line you want. You want to avoid side slipping with the front tire out of the rut and the rear tire in it, or worse yet, cross-rutting with both tires in two different ruts. Ruts can be ridden in either the sitting or standing position, but standing is better as you can more quickly shift or move to help the bike stay on line. In certain situations like riding through a gnarly rut section, whoops, and jumps, it is good practice to momentarily grip the bike with your legs to help control or stabilize it. Picking the right rut is sometimes the hardest part, and knowing when to try a different rut is what makes a winning rider. Remember, the rut you used in the beginning of a race will change every lap over the course of the race. Use caution when braking in deep ruts, and concentrate on getting your bike's lean angle correct for rutted turns.

How to practice motocross jumps

When you venture onto a motocross track, you will encounter a variety of jumps that will challenge you and require special techniques, depending on the speed and distance you're jumping. Typical motocross jumps include supercross-style jumps, which are short and steep, tabletop jumps, step-up and step-down jumps, double and triple jumps, and jumps with kickers in them. Kickers are often

a vertical lip of hard dirt on the last part of the jump face that if not taken aggressively can "kick" your rear end over or to the side and out of control. Pick your line carefully, and if you can't avoid a kicker, attack it and use it to gain additional elevation.

Your best approach when racing motocross is to take every jump seriously and commit. Sometimes the worst thing you can do is make a half-hearted attempt and let the bike and the jump decide where you'll end up. Regardless of the jump, the same basic things are critical. You must accelerate all the way up the face of a jump, and you must commit by carrying enough speed to clear the jump and not land on the flat or on the face of another jump. In motocross you don't have to jump every double or triple jump on the track, but if you ever want to take a first-place trophy home, you probably will eventually have to learn them. If you race, make sure you're in the right class. If others in your class are jumping the tough ones and you're not, that could be dangerous.

Advanced jumping techniques include landing with the front wheel first on a down slope. You can do that on big jumps by tapping the rear brake while airborne or on smaller jumps by chopping the throttle right after takeoff.

3 The more you can adapt to changing track conditions and switch to a new line as needed, ...

4 ...the better results you will get.

Seat bounces are when riders use their body weight to briefly bounce off the seat to compress the rear suspension right before takeoff and then spring with their legs when the suspension rebounds to get more altitude to clear a jump (gas it at the same time to get even more lift). Scrubbing is an advanced technique created by James "Bubba" Stewart; it is also called the Bubba Scrub. It is used when a rider suddenly leans his or her bike aggressively at the last minute on the approach to a jump in order to reduce the altitude and get the bike's tires back onto the ground to accelerate again.

Another motocross jumping technique is pre-jumping. Riders do this when they *don't* want to get much air off a jump, kind of like the Bubba Scrub. The way to pre-jump is to approach the jump as you normally would in the attack stance, except right before takeoff push all your weight down on the pegs and bars to compress the suspension as much as possible and then time it so you "hop" back up right at takeoff. If you do it right, you won't jump as high and can get back to the ground, where you can start accelerating more quickly than if you were flying through the air. This technique

Soft Bermed Turns

1 To tackle a soft bermed turn you must charge into it, then downshift and brake, sit down and forward, and extend your leg out in front.

2 At the last minute, release the brakes, ...

3 ...lean your bike into the berm, turn your handlebars slightly, clutch it, ...

4 ...and accelerate hard out of it.

sounds similar to the seat bounce described above, but they are different and have completely opposite goals. You can learn them simply by practicing and getting a feel for how each technique works.

Treat jumping just like any new skill you are learning. Constantly experiment and exaggerate when practicing jumping to gain a good perspective of what is too much and what is enough. Don't forget about hitting the throttle or brakes in the air to help alter the bike's attitude. Rev it more to get the front end higher, or shut off the throttle and use the rear brake to move the front end down. Proficient jumpers often use their legs at times to grab or squeeze their bikes to help them stabilize or control the bikes in the air as well. Constant practicing and gradually increasing the difficulty level as your control and confidence improves is never more important than it is when learning how to jump a motorcycle.

Hitting the Inside Line

1 The inside line is usually the most popular line and can become rutted like this.

2 Approach it standing and then drop into it and sit at the last minute, lock into it, ...

3 ...and immediately begin accelerating around the turn.

4 Don't lean too far back and make sure to commit to the corner by keeping your shoulders parallel with your handlebars.

21 Trials

"To ride a motorcycle seriously is to go nowhere fast."

The great quote above is from the book *Art of the Motorcycle*, from the Guggenheim Museum motorcycle exhibit. I feel it is a spot-on description of what trials riders do. The reason we've included this chapter about specialized trials motorcycle riding is because we believe, and most experts agree, that riding and practicing trials is one of the best ways to learn maximum motorcycle control techniques that will improve your off-road (and overall) motorcycle-riding skills. There's also the fact that trials bikes are a lot of fun to ride.

Trials riders are a special breed of off-road rider who thrive on extreme challenges and are rarely satisfied. Good trials riders can make something that is difficult look easy, but of course it's not. It's their attention to the smallest details, and tons of practice, that allows them to make something hard to do look effortless.

The following is a brief background about the unique trials motorcycles, the challenging sport of observed trials competition, the valuable benefits of riding trials to all motorcyclists, and some basic specialized techniques that are used in trials. Master the basic exercises in this book and the basic trials riding skills in this chapter and you'll be ready for more advanced trials training and coaching. After riding a trials bike for a while you'll be amazed at how easily you can now ride through gnarly terrain on your dirt bike or dual-sport that was unthinkable to ride through before.

"A strong trials background will give you the ability to ride any type of motorsport. The technical skills inherited from riding trials carry over to any other type of motorcycle discipline. When riding trials, you become one with the bike. Your clutch, brake, throttle control, and body positioning will be perfected and will help you with whatever type of motorcycle riding you prefer. I would highly recommend purchasing a trials bike to help hone your riding abilities."

Cody Webb

2002 AMA National High School Class Trials champion, 2003 AMA National Expert Trials champion, 2007 and 2008 AMA Indoor National Trials champion, 2010 AMA National Trials champion

Trials bikes are to motorcycling what rock-crawlers are to four-wheelers. They are small and have modest horse-power, but are light and designed to accelerate quickly, sometimes straight up a wall. Just like today's motocross bikes, trials bikes are purpose-built, no-frills, competition machines, which are becoming even more specialized as time goes on. Trials bikes are designed for a specific purpose: to carry their riders through a marked section of difficult obstacles.

In trials competition, riders go one at a time and are constantly watched by judges as they navigate through a marked course filled with seemingly impossible obstacles (both natural and manmade). Their primary goal is to always stay in bounds and to avoid putting their feet on the ground (dabbing), or at the worst, stalling, falling, or tipping over. The rider gets a penalty point for every mistake. At the end of the day, the rider with the fewest penalty points wins.

Unfortunately, trials bikes aren't offered in most motor-cycle retailers and used trials bikes are even harder to find. The best source for a new or used trials bike is your local trials riding club. One member may be ready to upgrade and is willing to sell you his bike, while another member might be a "garage dealer" of one brand or another and would be happy to order a new one for you. Current brands include Gas Gas (Spain), Sherco (Spain), Beta (Italian), Montessa (Spain), Ossa (Spain), and Scorpa (France).

Trials riding gear is different from off-road riding gear. It is much lighter, which reflects the slower speeds of trials.

Trials riders sometimes walk and hike as much as ride. Serious trials competitors will wear tight-fitting low-resistance pants and jerseys, lightweight gloves, an open-face helmet, and lightweight boots with aggressive hiking soles. Recreational trials riders will often simply wear off-road or motocross pants and jerseys along with a trials helmet and boots.

Trials motorcycles are designed to be ridden while standing up only, making them a real challenge for most beginners. We recommend that beginners learn to ride a dirt bike first where they can sit down and put at least one foot on the ground while sitting before trying a trials bike. But as soon as they are somewhat comfortable with riding a dirt bike standing up, they are ready to take a trials bike for a spin. The only time you sit on a trials bike is when you are sitting still. Because the only way to ride a trials bike is standing up, it forces you to learn how to ride in the attack position or the energy conservation mode. It also shows you how you can shift your weight around and actually steer the bike with your lower body and how to "dab" or put your foot down correctly while riding in order to keep your balance and remain upright, among many other valuable riding habits. Riding trials is physically demanding. Trials riders have often been described as the gymnasts of motorcycling.

Trials competition tests your ability to ride your bike over technical terrain without losing penalty points. They are not about who goes the fastest and crosses the finish line first as in motocross. Competing in a trials event can be frustrating at first because you are being scored and must keep your feet up and stay in bounds. For anyone new to trials, we recommend that you play ride on a trials bike for a while, and if you like it and really want to get better at it, then try some trials competition. That's when your skills will improve quickly. You'll find that trials competitors are typically happy to lend advice, because they know it's entirely up to you to use the techniques needed to conquer a tough trials section. The sport of trials is extreme off-road riding at its best and a popular, well-respected international motorsport, but many people simply enjoy play riding on trials bikes at their local riding areas. Unfortunately, trials competitions are not promoted well and are usually held in remote locations, which makes it discouraging for the average rider to venture out and see one.

For kids, trials riding is an ideal way to build their technical fundamentals in a relatively safe way so that speed becomes a tool to be used as needed, not the only thing they know how to do. Low-speed skills can be harder to develop than high-speed skills and may be frustrating for

The Roll-Up

1 The roll-up is the most common trials climbing technique.

2 It involves wheelying into the top portion of an obstacle and using it to help the bike "roll up" and...

3 ...over it without hitting the skid plate.

4 This expert-level technique can be used by off-roaders and dual sport riders too.

some people. If you ask a kid what he or she wants to do, the kid will usually say motocross because that's all they see in the magazines and on TV.

Unfortunately, most kids don't know about trials or have access to it or they would probably like to try it too. Parents have control over what their kids do while they're young, which is a great time to give them some trials experience before moving on to a speed sport if that is ultimately what they want to do. With trials, kids will learn to walk before they run and will be more prepared for a variety of riding challenges.

If you don't own a trials bike yet, you can still practice trials techniques on your conventional dirt bike. Of course, there's nothing like using the right tool for the job to speed up the learning process. Riding trials will develop your technical motorcycle riding skills better than anything else. Trials bikes are so light, willing, and capable, you'll have the confidence to try challenging terrain, knowing that if you crash or get stuck you can physically lift the light bike out of trouble. The bike's slight weight makes it very responsive to a rider's input. The bike gives you immediate feedback if you're doing it right or wrong. Riding a trials bike teaches how much you can move your body to help your bike and how correct body positioning will make all the difference. Riding trials teaches how to maximize clutch use, how to develop front brake feel, how to climb, descend, and turn, the importance of rear-wheel awareness, how to read terrain and pick good lines, how you can use several controls simultaneously, how to tread lightly and identify traction zones and no-traction zones, and how to ride better than those people who don't know trials.

As a testament to the real value of trials, simply look at most of the outstanding off-road motorcycle racers, especially those competing in the new AMA National Endurocross Series and you'll discover a common trait: They either have a background in trials or they naturally think and ride like a trials rider. Trials riding can be very physical and many professional motorcycle racers are now using trials for cross-training, while experienced riders are always amazed at how their skills have improved after riding trials. This may be just what you have been looking for to give you an advantage.

If you want to try trials, you can try the following:
• Borrow a trials bike from a friend or trials club member.
• Purchase a new trials bike from a dealer or a used trials bike if you can find one.
• Come out to MotoVentures' private trials riding paradise in California for a day of riding a late-model trials bike

and receive training on all the important basic trials riding fundamentals.

How to practice key trials riding techniques

News trials riders will want to learn and practice a few specialized trials techniques. Keep in mind when practicing trials, the object is to ride as cleanly as possible by not footing, falling, or going out of bounds. Climbing steep hills and uphill jumping on a trials bike is fun and skill building, but doesn't represent a typical trials section. These are usually tight, technical, well marked, and designed to be difficult and draw penalty points.

Your first goal is to become comfortable with using all the controls, often using more than one at the same time. You want to become comfortable with using the clutch and front brake with one finger while hanging on and twisting the throttle. Get comfortable with riding so slowly, or stopping, that you have to use the clutch a lot while maintaining your balance. Learn how to stop and rest and balance comfortably with your feet up, and learn how to ride in either the attack position or the energy conservation mode.

Next, concentrate on perfecting your counterbalancing skills. Turning a trials bike also includes practicing a sideways hop in both directions and with both front and rear wheels so you can make tighter turns in confined spaces. Hopping sideways a few inches at a time involves lots of arm and leg springing coupled with a slight movement (lean) in the direction you wish to move. First learn to hop the front then learn to hop the rear.

After that, here are four climbing techniques you will want to master: the bunny hop, the roll-up, the zap, and the splatter. Really good riders can actually use these extreme trials techniques when riding their dirt bikes too.

The bunny hop

To practice a bunny hop, simply place a small object like a rock in a flat, open area, and ride over it in first gear without touching it with either tire. The technique is to pop a wheelie over the object and just before your rear tire gets to it, shut off the throttle. Using your legs, rapidly transfer your weight forward to unload the rebounding rear suspension and tire. This helps lift the rear tire off the ground and over the object. This exercise really helps develop your rear-wheel awareness. It is essential to know where your rear tire is at all times and to be able to help it climb steps by transferring your weight at the right time. For fun, we use empty aluminum soda cans or plastic water bottles. That way, if you don't do it right, you'll have a crushed can or bottle.

The roll-up

To practice a roll-up, locate a small rock or log that is just big enough for your skid plate to scrape if you roll over it. In first gear, approach the object, and just before you get to it, pop a wheelie, but instead of placing your front tire on top of the object, punch it into the top third and use the rock or log to "roll up" or bounce off it to create an even bigger wheelie at the moment just before your rear tire hits it. Performing a roll up will create more clearance so your skid plate won't contact the object, and you will be able to ride over larger obstacles with ease. Roll-ups are the climbing technique that Enduro-X racers use to ride their fast bikes over giant obstacles on those gnarly courses.

The Zap

1 Performing a zap will come in handy for crossing little gaps and climbing up undercut ledges like this one.

2 To zap something you must wheelie and punch your front tire into the top part of the obstacle.

3 At the moment your front tire hits the object, momentarily clutch the engine to raise the rpms, then release the clutch and spring with your legs as the suspension also rebounds, ...

4 ...which will launch you and your bike to the top of the rock.

The zap

To practice a zap, locate a modestly-size rock with an undercut ledge or no face for your rear tire to climb up. Approach it just as you would in a roll-up wheelie, except punch the front tire into the top quarter of the rock even harder while momentarily pulling in the clutch to quickly raise the rpm, then release it while springing upward with your legs as your compressed suspension rebounds and your clutch releases. This physical move will result in your rear tire jumping from where it was last on the ground when the front tire touched rock to where the front tire first touched the rock, avoiding any contact with the faceless, undercut rock. This is the seemingly magic technique that pros use to climb up difficult rocks and to leap across small gaps.

The splatter

To practice a splatter, you must have guts, and nerves of steel—and a good minder or spotter to catch your bike wouldn't hurt either. When a rider can't quite make it up a big splatter, his minder can grab the bike, saving it and the rider,

The Splatter

1 Splatters are used for climbing objects too tall to roll up or zap.

2 Splatters are the triple jumps of trials and require that you accelerate hard in second or third gear, then wheelie and also use a small rock if you can to help you get airborne.

who is too busy saving himself to worry about his bike falling on top of him.

To practice a splatter, start with a modestly tall rock that is too tall to roll up or zap. Find a helper rock and place it a few feet away, depending on the height of the climb. Approach the climb aggressively in second or even third gear, then pull in the clutch to rev the engine and release the clutch while using the helper rock to initiate the wheelie. Use the helper rock as a ramp to launch the rear wheel while you pull back hard on the handlebars. Between the sudden

acceleration, the rock ramp, and you pulling back on the handlebars, you will rotate backward as you fly through the air, just enough to help you contact the vertical rock face with the rear tire first, a greater distance up the rock than you would with any other technique. Perform it correctly and your momentum and traction from the rear tire will carry you up the last few feet and over the top. Splatters are the technique that enables top trials riders to climb seemingly impossible tall vertical climbs. A splatter is to a trials rider what a triple jump is to a motocross rider.

3 In the air you must over-rotate backward so your rear tire contacts the object first.

4 Your momentum and some traction from the rear tire hitting the object will do the rest.

GLOSSARY OF TERMS

Apex: The point in a turn where you are the closest to the inside of the turn. Move your apex later in the turn and make a "late apex," move it earlier in the turn and it's an "early apex."

Arm pump: When your forearms swell up while riding hard, making it hard to hang on. It can usually be treated with proper conditioning, the correct diet, and complete hydration.

ATV: All-Terrain Vehicle, aka four-wheeler or quad.

Back it in: Sliding the rear tire to help turn the bike, either under power or braking, while entering a turn.

Balance wheelie: Describes a wheelie where the bike is standing almost vertically on its rear wheel at or near the balance point of going over backward.

Barkbusters: Guards to protect your hands/handlebars and allow you to ride through tight trees without hitting your hands, hence the name "barkbusters."

Berms: Ridges of dirt that are built up on the outside of turns from riders sliding into the corner.

Berm shot: Describes the quick execution of a bermed turn on a motocross track.

Blip (the throttle): A quick twist of the throttle.

Blockpass: When you turn inside a competitor ahead of you while in a turn and get in front or block him at the turn exit.

Bog (the engine): What happens when you let the RPMs get too low.

Bottleneck: Where the trail narrows down, forcing racers to follow single file to get through. If someone in front stops or gets stuck, it creates a "bottleneck jam."

Bottom-out: When your suspension reaches its limits of full compression.

Brakeslide: Locking up the rear brake at a turn entrance to help rotate the bike.

Bulldog: Technique used to ride down an extremely steep hill. Picture a cowboy wrestling a steer.

Bumpstart: Starting your bike by letting it roll downhill and releasing the clutch with the bike in gear, which turns over the engine to start it.

Bunny hop: The technique used to lift your rear tire off the ground to hop over something while riding.

Butt steer: What happens when you hit a bump while sitting down and the jolt transfers through your body and causes you to steer in the wrong direction with your arms.

Case it: Hitting your bike's skid plate (undercarriage) on a jump, rock, log, etc., when going over it.

Centipede: What you look like when you push with both feet while riding sitting down trying to not get stuck in a tough section.

Cheater sand: Sand that is wet and firm, providing great traction.

Chop the throttle: To shut the throttle off very quickly or abruptly.

Class: Motorcycle races have many competition "classes" for different sized bikes, rider skills, and even age groups.

Clutch it: To slightly pull in or "slip the clutch" to momentarily hesitate or to gain engine rpms for more power.

Counterbalancing: Leaning the bike while standing at low speeds and counterbalancing with your body in the opposite direction to keep from falling over.

Cow trailing: Following paths originally made by cows and other animals.

Cross-grain: Describes when you must ride off-camber on a sidehill course that is 90 degrees from the direction water flows downhill. Cross-grain trails are usually technical and tough to ride.

Cross-rut: Having your front and rear wheels in two different parallel ruts at the same time.

Cross-up: When your bike is pointed one way and your shoulders are pointed the other. This also describes one of the first FMX tricks invented by World Motocross Champion Roger DeCoster, where he twisted his handlebars and leaned his bike sideways in midair.

Dab: A trials term used for when a rider puts a foot down to regain his or her balance, picking up penalty points in the process.

Damping: The term used to describe your front or rear suspension adjustments that help control the compression or rebound motions of your suspension. Often incorrectly called "dampening."

Double jump: Using one jump to catch air, then landing on the downside of a second jump.

Doughnut: The act of spinning a tight 360-degree circle.

Dual-Sport: a.k.a., Dual Purpose. Describes motorcycles that are used for both street riding and dirt riding.

Endo: Short for end-over-end, which describes what happens when a bike suddenly slows or stops and the rider is bucked or pitched over the handlebars.

Enduro: Rugged off-road races that also require time-keeping skills to avoid arriving too early. Also describes a motorcycle used for off-road riding.

Endurocross: The newest form of off-road motorcycle racing which involves racing around a course built in small stadiums and arenas that are full of challenging obstacles.

Fade: Describes when your energy level drops while riding and you start slowing down. Fading is dangerous and can be avoided with a proper diet and exercise.

Fan the clutch: To rapidly pull the clutch lever in and out to raise the engine rpms.

Fixate: When you look at an obstacle on the trail for too long and end up hitting it. Also known as "target fixation."

Flat tracking: Powersliding around an oval, usually turning left. Also describes racing around an oval.

Flick the clutch: see *Fan the clutch.*

Flying W: When you hit a bump you didn't see at speed and the seat hits your butt and throws your feet up over your head, which looks like a flying W from behind.

FMX: Freestyle Motocross, which is the sport of performing extreme tricks off of jumps.

Four-stroke engine: aka Thumper. Produces a smooth, broad power, but is heavier, more expensive, and harder to maintain. Pollutes less than a two-stroke.

Friction zone: The point in the process of releasing the clutch where the bike begins to move forward.

Full-lock: When your front forks (and handlebars) are turned as far as they can go (locked) to the right or left.

Garage dealer: Someone who sells motorcycles from his house and doesn't have a retail store.

Ghost ride: When a rider steps off his or her bike on purpose while moving to launch it up, into, or over something.

G-out: What happens when you ride downhill, hit the bottom, and suddenly start uphill, causing your suspension to bottom out.

Handling: Describes how good (or bad) your bike works when riding over tough terrain.

Headshake: aka, Speed Wobble. When your handlebars violently swap left and right, which is often due to poor chassis and/or suspension set-up.

Hero dirt: Dirt that has the perfect amount of traction in it.

Highcenter: What happens when your skid plate gets hung up when riding over on a log or rock and your rear tire spins helplessly in the air.

High side: Crashing as your bike flops over to the outside of a turn, instead of the inside. The rider is usually flung through the air and rewarded with a harsh landing.

Holeshot: In motocross, a holeshot is when you win the race into the first turn after the start.

Hook-up: When your rear tire starts to get traction when accelerating.

Jetting: Describes installing the correct "jets" in your engine's carburetor to make your bike run correctly or to compensate for change in altitude. Jetting will be a

thing of the past when bikes start coming with computer-controlled fuel injection.

Kicker: A lip or ledge on a jump that will kick your rear end out of control if you're not careful.

Knobbies: Describes the tread or bumps on off-road or motocross tires, also used to describe the tires.

Lane racing: When two riders ride briskly together down a two-track road, each keeping in their own lane.

Line: The narrow and specific path you are trying to follow with your tires.

Lip: Describes the last foot or two of a jump that is often vertical and could cause you to jump even higher or could kick you sideways or end-over-end.

Loop out: What happens when you flip over backward while climbing a hill or doing a wheelie.

Lose it: Describes the feeling when the front or back tire suddenly loses traction.

Low side: Crashing by laying the bike down to the low side of the bike instead of the high side. This is one of the most common mistakes you can make while turning a motorcycle and, fortunately, rarely hurts the bike or rider.

Lug: When your engine rpms are too low for the gear you're in or the speed you're going.

Manuel: Technique of riding a stand-up wheelie over an obstacle like whoop-dedoos. Named after the BMX star who originated it.

Marbles: Loose rocks the size of marbles, lots of fun (not) to ride on!

Minder: A person who rides with a professional trials rider with the primary job of catching the rider's bike in a crash to help save both the bike and the rider from getting hit by the bike!

Mini-bike: A small dirt bike.

Monkey-Butt: A rash or raw skin "down there" from riding too much. Wearing riding shorts will help.

Moto: A motocross race, usually two races per class in each event.

Moto-goon: Someone who rides a motocross bike but isn't a very good rider.

Muscle memory: What happens when you practice perfectly and your muscles remember so they can repeat.

Nose wheelie: aka, Stoppie. It's what happens when you stop or slow down so abruptly with the front brake that the rear wheel rises in the air and you ride a front wheel wheelie for a while.

Numb butt: (1) No feeling in your butt from riding so much. (2) A person who cannot tell you how their bike is performing so you can tune it for them.

Off-camber: A sidehill or off-camber route that is not straight up or down a hill.

Overbalanced: What happens when you're trying really hard to keep your balance and you lose it.

Over the bars: see also Endo. When your body flips over the front of your bike.

Over your head: Riding too fast for your skills, looking sketchy, out of control, etc.

Pinned: Holding the throttle wide open as if a steel pin was inserted to lock open the throttle.

Pivot turn: Spinning or flipping your bike around quickly from a standing start to go in the other direction.

Planed out: When your bike reaches the right speed in sand or mud and begins to easily ride over it as opposed to digging into it.

Powerband: The rpm range where your engine is producing the most power.

Powerslide: What happens in a turn when you lean the bike and apply power, causing the rear tire to spin and help you rotate the bike around.

Power wheelie: When you use only acceleration or power (instead of balance) to keep the front wheel in the air.

Pressurizing: Weighting or loading your foot pegs and/or handlebars with your arms/hands and legs/feet.

Pulsating: Squeezing and releasing the front brake when you haven't developed the feel to hold it steady.

Push: What happens in a turn when your front tire washes out or pushes while you're riding aggressively.

Rail: When a rider is riding fast around a turn with his wheels locked in line as if "on a rail."

Rear steer: Steering your motorcycle by powersliding it around a turn.

Rear-wheel awareness: Knowing exactly where the rear wheel is so you can time your leg spring/absorb.

Rebound: Your suspension moving upward or rebounding following compression of the spring(s).

Revs, rpms: Your engine's revolutions per minute. Roughly speaking, higher rpm means more power.

Rock clipping: The act of clipping a small rock with your rear tire, causing it to fling your rear wheel sideways, usually out of control.

Rock gardens: A trail filled with rocks of a variety of sizes and shapes, both firm and loose.

Roller: Small to mid-size rocks (or logs) that are not firmly planted and move when you ride over them.

Roll-up: A trials technique for climbing small to medium rocks, which can also be used by trail riders.

Roost(ed): Roost is the dirt and rock spray that flies off your spinning rear tire. Don't get roosted.

Ruts: Erosion in the ground usually caused by rain or running water.

Sag: The amount of slack or free play in your bike's suspension.

Scrubbing: A motocross technique where a rider suddenly leans their bike on the face of a jump ramp in order to reduce their altitude in the air and get back on the ground to accelerate again. Invented by James "Bubba" Stewart and often referred to as doing the Bubba Scrub.

Section: In trials competition, a section is a piece of terrain with marked boundaries where the competitors are scored.

Setup: Placing or adjusting your bike's controls and suspension settings to suit your weight, skill, and preferences.

Short shift: The act of shifting up one more gear than is optimum to lower the engine rpms for smoother, more controllable acceleration and deceleration.

Singletrack: A narrow one-lane motorcycle or mountain bike trail—some of the most fun off-road riding you can do.

Sketchy: Out-of-control riding, always taking chances, a crash waiting to happen . . .

Skid plate: A metal or plastic plate located under your engine to skid over dirt, rocks, logs, etc.

Sling shot: Describes the action of rocking the bike back and forth and releasing the clutch to get unstuck.

Snake bite: When you get a flat tire by pinching the tube in two places, like a snake bite, from hitting a hard surface too fast or by running insufficient tire air pressure.

Soil sample: Crashing.

Spit back: When a four-stroke engine quits suddenly, usually from incorrect jetting or temperatures.

Splatter: A trials technique used for climbing a tall, vertical face by launching into it rear wheel first.

Squid: A person who pit races or acts inappropriately on a motorcycle.

Stoppie: aka, Nose Wheelie. The act of stopping so quickly the rear tire comes off the ground.

SuperCross: Indoor motocross usually held in large sports stadiums.

Swap: Short for swapping ends, which is when your rear wheel violently swaps back and forth, usually while riding fast through a set of nasty whoops.

Sweep rider: The person who rides last and never passes anyone to make sure nobody is left behind.

Switch back trail: A switch back trail ascends/descends a steep slope that has tight turns to "switch back" and go the other way. Switch back trail turns are tight and challenging, especially downhill right-handers.

Tank slap: When your bike's forks flop left and right violently against the steering stops, looking like they are slapping each side of the gas tank.

Threshold: When braking hard, the threshold is the point just before the tire locks up and skids.

Throttle happy: Erratic use of the throttle or twisting the grip too rapidly.

Tire irons: Tools needed to remove or mount new tires on your wheels or to fix a flat tire.

Trail braking: Applying the brakes slightly, especially the rear brake, while entering a turn to help rotate the bike.

Tread lightly: A way of riding off-road that minimizes your impact on the environment.

Trials: Specialized, highly technical form of motorcycle competition that is scored by points deducted rather than speed.

Triple jump: Using one jump to completely clear a second jump and land on the downslope of a third jump.

Two-stroke engine: aka, Ring Ding. Has a high power-to-weight ratio, is easy to maintain, repair, and upgrade, but unfortunately emits more pollution than a four-stroke.

Two-track: Two-track roads are formed from four-wheel vehicles leaving a margin in the middle, forcing motorcycles to ride in one track or the other.

Understeer: Turning your handlebars even tighter while in a turn, causing the front tire to skid sideways slightly, making you run wide in the turn.

Velocitized: After traveling at speed for a while, one can become "velocitized" and underestimate how long it will take to slow down and stop, like when you must stop at the bottom of a freeway off-ramp.

Washed out: When your front tire loses traction in a turn and causes you to crash.

Wheelie: Lifting your front tire while accelerating— used to skim over obstacles or just to show off.

Whiskey throttle: Describes when your bike accelerates and you're not ready for it and it pulls your body back, including your right arm and wrist, and you can't shut off the throttle.

Zap: A trials riding technique for climbing medium height undercut rocks and ledges.

INDEX

ABOUT THE AUTHOR

Gary LaPlante has over 43 years of experience riding, racing, testing, and working on a wide variety of motorcycles. During that time, Gary developed excellent teaching and communication skills from over 30 years of working in key positions in the motorcycle industry and over 12 years' experience of personally teaching riders almost every week while operating MotoVentures Inc., offering tours, training, and trials services in Anza, California. Gary's diversity of technical riding skills and wide range of professional experience has enabled him to create his own teaching curriculums, which is what this book is based upon. Gary has a true passion and enthusiasm for motorcycling and has dedicated his life to studying and practicing the art of riding motorcycles well. *How to Ride Off-Road Motorcycles* contains everything Gary has learned and experienced first-hand by riding, working on, or writing about a wide variety of motorcycles, especially off-road, motocross, and trials motorcycles, for almost his entire life.

ABOUT MOTOVENTURES

MotoVentures operates a full-time training operation year-round from a private, ideally suited, 350-acre Rider Training Center located near the town of Anza in southern California. MotoVentures utilizes dirt bikes to teach motorcycle riding skills and offers five different motorcycle rider training curriculums: Level 1 for beginners, Level 2 for novice to advanced, Level 3 for advanced, Specialized Trials Training, and Motocross 101 Training. MotoVentures has trained thousands of riders since starting in 1998 and enjoys an unmatched reputation for high-quality services and true professionalism. Attending a MotoVentures motorcycle rider training course will have you learning how to ride right, right from the beginning. For more information about MotoVentures rider-training courses, go to MotoVentures .com or call toll-free: (877) 260-MOTO.

ACKNOWLEDGMENTS

This book has been one of the most challenging things I have ever accomplished, and it wouldn't have happened without a lot of help and encouragement from many great people. The fact is, I started writing it for my instructors: my son, Andre, Rob Hock, Brandon Hamlett (my three main photo models), and others who instruct for me so they can teach exactly what I want taught. They are the future of MotoVentures. First thanks go to My Men.

Next, I owe a big thank-you to my faithful customers who are the actual intended audience for this book. They have trusted me over the past 13 years to perform "as advertised" and in the process helped me hone my curriculums, teaching techniques, and communication skills, giving me the information I needed to write this book.

I owe a big thank-you to all those directly involved with producing this book: Bobbie Carlson, Kevin Krasner, and Wally Trevains at Cape Fox, the first outsiders to read my "Practice Guide" in 2011 and encourage me to get it published. Thanks to Zack Miller at MBI Publishing Company for pulling my book from his over-stuffed inbox and actually reading it, and thanks to my editor, Steve Casper, for putting up with my protests and helping me through "the process."

Big thanks go to all those Top Pros who contributed: Keith Code, Scott Hoffman, Eric Storz, Eric Bostrom, Kerry Peterson, Andy Leisner, Fred Andrews, Cory Graffunder, Jonah Street, Mark Cernicky, Dave Pyle, Ty Davis, Johnny Murfree, Gary Jones, Lee Parks, Ken Faught, Paul Thede, Geoff Aaron, Cody Webb, Tim Morton, Brian Catterson, Fred Hoess, Andy Jefferson, Ron Lawson, and Jeff Tilton.

I am also very fortunate to have a special group of industry friends and sponsors to thank: Mike Cline (Matrix), Hector Cademartori (Artist), Tom Hicks (Motorcycle Dealer), David Docktor (Yamaha), Corey Eastman (Husqvarna), Mark Gandy (HJC & TCX), Greg Blackwell (Parts Unlimited), Brent Durfee (Dunlop), Ernie Soliz (Torco), and Paul Thede (Race Tech).

Finally, of course, I must thank my family, who always stands behind me through thick and thin: my brother Ed and his wife, Donna (my "Advertising Agency"), to my mother, Lydia, my son, Andre, and last, but most importantly, a very special thank-you to my loving and incredibly supportive girlfriend, Cynthia.

PHOTO CREDITS

Scott Hoffman/JA Media Group
pages 106, 154

National Off-Highway Vehicle Conservation Council
pages 22, 30, 68, 98, 138

Yamaha Motor Corporation
pages 56, 64, 110, 116, 144, 150